MAKE YOUR CHILD
A WINNER

'The book is full of no-nonsense examples to illustrate the points the author wants to make. A good addition to your childcare library.'
– *Femina*

'Dr Pradeep Kapoor addresses various concerns of parents and gives bounteous guidance in a manner only a professional, in this case a Pediatrician, can. The book is a psychological treatise on parent-child relationship rather than a handbook on off-hand tips on parenting.'
– *The Tribune on Sunday*

'Dr Pradeep Kapoor, in his book *Make Your Child A Winner* gives ample tips to replace tentative experimentation with well-informed parenting methodology.'
– *The New Indian Express*

'The book *Make Your Child A Winner* written by Dr Pradeep Kapoor, a Bhopal-based Pediatrician, is a comprehensive effort in providing Indian parents with an Indian perspective.'
– *Central Chronicle*

MAKE YOUR CHILD A WINNER

Dr Pradeep Kapoor

Rupa . Co

Copyright © Pradeep Kapoor 2002

First Published 2002
Sixth Impression 2011

Published by
Rupa Publications India Pvt. Ltd.
7/16, Ansari Road, Daryaganj,
New Delhi 110 002

Sales Centres:

Allahabad Bengaluru Chennai
Hyderabad Jaipur Kathmandu
Kolkata Mumbai

All rights reserved.
No part of this publication may be reproduced, stored in a
retrieval system, or transmitted, in any form or by any means,
electronic, mechanical, photocopying, recording or otherwise,
without the prior permission of the publishers.

The author asserts the moral right to be identified
as the author of this work.

Typeset in 11 pt. Zapf Elliptical by
Mindways Design
1410 Chiranjiv Tower
43 Nehru Place
New Delhi 110 019

Printed in India by
Rekha Printers Pvt. Ltd.
A-102/1, Okhla Industrial Area, Phase-II
New Delhi 110 020

To my daughters Misha and Zoya
For teaching me that–
Every child in some respects is like all other children,
but in some, he or she is like no other.

Contents

Introduction	*ix*
Acknowledgements	*xi*
Author's Note	*xiii*
Every Child is Born–A Winner	1
From Nobody to Somebody	17
The Struggles of Childhood	32
Home: The Base Camp	42
School: The Battle Ground	60
The Problem Child	80
The Abused Child	99
Illness can Undermine Self-esteem	113
Combating Inferiority Complex	136
All Children Have Fears	148
Every Child is Unique	159
Do you Shout too Much?	167
Good Parents Communicate Better	179
A Born Leader?	188
The Horror Called-Homework	197
Friends are Important	206

Smart Parenting	215
Are You a Good Father?	226
Teachers Teach-Hobbies Educate	241
Reach For The Moon	249

Introduction

Parenting is an art, which relies heavily on the use of common sense. It is serious business, hence you will find serious and animated discussion in some chapters. It is fun, so be ready for entertaining pieces. It is gratifying, rest assured reading this book would be a fulfilling experience. Don't look for gems of wisdom, try to discover the common sense, which is lurking behind each sentence of this book.

Growing children are full of exuberant curiosity and vitality. If they get a nurturing environment throughout the crucial growing-up period, they develop into winners. If during this decisive period they face failure or rejection, the result is a collapse of confidence and withdrawal from the struggle towards worthwhile achievement. Such children suffer from insecurities and have doubts about the self.

Self-esteem and success are directly related to each other. Children who grow up feeling good about themselves, who are made to feel that they are worthwhile people and who enjoy warm and satisfying relationships with their parents, teachers and peers, usually do well in life. We must ensure that children do not suffer unnecessary mental, emotional or physical trauma that may damage their self-esteem and undermine their potential.

The most important developmental task in childhood is the acquisition of self-confidence, emotional stability and a balanced way of dealing with life's challenges and frustrations. Parents serve as the primary role models for their children. They must respond empathetically to the critical developmental needs of their children. Parents who are themselves confident achievers find it easy to motivate their children to strive for excellence.

In most cases, parents use a trial and error method while dealing with their children. Through this book an attempt has been made to replace this tentative experimentation with well-informed parenting methodology. Undoubtedly, success comes at a premium, but care must be taken that it is not achieved at the cost of a warm and loving relationship with your child.

Who should read this book? Anyone and everyone: who interacts with children, whether as a parent, grandparent, teacher or relative. All parents want their children to excel and become successful in life. This is only possible if they eliminate weaknesses and reinforce the strengths of their wards. This book is intended to help these very endeavours of parents. On one hand the book aims to bring new insight, on the other it tries to reconfirm the good practices already present in our society. Let us join hands to ensure that all children get optimal love, care and guidance at home, at school and in society.

Pradeep Kapoor

Acknowledgements

The first person I must acknowledge is no more with me. The dedication and devotion of my grandmother towards my career and my success, I still find truly amazing. My parents gave me my moorings, my bearings and ample opportunities to grow and develop optimally. Sending me to The Scindia School, Gwalior to study being one of them.

I had read somewhere, 'Behind every successful man, is a surprised woman!' I know, this is not the case with my wife Dr Neelkamal, who was always by my side—not behind. She is largely responsible for my evolution as a doctor, father, author, and above all as a human being. Her insight as a medical person and her foresight as a mother, provided me with the vision to write this book.

Mrs. Prabha Tandon, my mother-in-law, a teacher with remarkable child counselling capabilities provided several interesting inputs, some of which have been incorporated as case studies in this book.

I will always remain indebted to my teacher, Dr. V.J. Rajput, who taught me the tricks of pediatric trade. He is not only an excellent clinician but an even better 'whistler'. I use his 'whistling technique' to great effect, to entertain/disarm my little patients before examining them.

I am grateful to Sumit Roy, Clinical-Psychologist, for his guidance and support at every step. N. Thomas who typed the manuscript, has never been invited to K.B.C. to play fastest-fingers-first with Mr. Amitabh Bachchan—I am sure he will win hands down. I would like to especially thank Ajay Chourasia, an enthusiastic computer professional, for helping me with the preparation of the manuscript. I am also thankful to Dr Mohammad Ali Husainy, Dr Rajeev Madan, Dr Renu Mishra, Dr Alka Tiwari and Mr. Ashok K Mondal who helped me in the making of this book. Finally, no author can deliver, and no book can be born without the faith of the publishers.

Author's Note

All names used in this book are fictitious; the episodes are real. Resemblance to any real people of those names is purely co-incidental and totally unintentional.

1

Every Child is born—A Winner

Life's aspirations come in the guise of children.
—Rabindranath Tagore

Birth of a child is an unforgettable moment for the family. Proud and fulfilled parents return home from the hospital with their 'bundle of joy', feeling at the top of the world. Festivities begin and never seem to end.

Where babies are concerned parents and especially mothers seem to have a keen eye, maybe a bit too keen. Lack of knowledge of normal development in a child gets them worked up and running to their doctor. To avoid this, parents should make themselves aware of the basics of the developmental process of a child.

The human newborn baby has the slowest rate of growth and development among mammals. Therefore, he or she is at the mercy of the parents or caretakers for a prolonged period of time.

Look carefully at your baby. Which is the most prominent part of its body? No, not hands or legs, neither chest nor abdomen and most definitely not the neck, which is the most indiscernible part of a baby. The most conspicuous part is the head and it contains the most exceptional apparatus in the universe: the human brain.

Probably the unique aspect of our human inheritance is a superior brain, which has ensured the supremacy and dominance of human race on earth. It consists of billions of nerve cells with countless interconnecting pathways. Through an elaborate and complex network of nerves, it controls the functioning of the rest of the body. Thus, the human brain provides a highly organised communication and computing network which can store experiences, solve problems and has the capabilities of imagining, reasoning and decision making.

Maturation of brain is a continuous process, which starts at conception, but gathers momentum after birth. Various milestones achieved by the child, in other words, the entire developmental process, is a direct consequence of the maturing brain.

The early developmental process provides the child with linguistic and social skills in addition to hand and body co-ordination. A basic knowledge of the important developmental milestones will allow the parents to know whether their child is growing normally or not. Parents need to be very cautious in becoming overly anxious because their child did not reach a specific milestone at a given age. If they have any concerns about their child's development, they should contact their pediatrician or a child psychologist: the right persons to evaluate his performance. This can help in early detection of any abnormality, prompt search for the probable cause and timely intervention. Knowledge of normal development will also assure the parents that their child is as good as other children and it is now in their hands to turn him into a winner.

The sequence of development is the same in all children, but the rate varies from child to child. For example, children have to learn to sit before they can walk, but the age at which different children learn to sit and to walk varies considerably. Similarly, children have to first produce vowel and consonant sounds, before they can speak words and full sentences, but again the age at which different children accomplish this varies greatly. The outcome of developmental process is governed by the nature/nurture principle i.e. the genetic make-up of the child and the environmental influences.

The Newborn (Birth to Four Weeks)

In medical jargon, your 'bundle of joy' is called a newborn during the initial four weeks of life. Newborns spend much of their time sleeping and feeding. They cry when they need to be fed, changed or held. This cry is their method of communication; it is the only language they know.

Your baby should be sucking and swallowing well. Start talking to your baby as early as possible, feeding time is ideal for doing this. A baby's neck muscles are weak, so always support the head gently. Provide as much physical contact as possible. All babies like to be comforted and need a lot of attention in order to grow strong and healthy.

One to Three Months

During this period babies become increasingly responsive. They react to sudden movements or noises, follow moving objects with eyes and appear to stare at you. They make cooing sounds and smile when played with. Around three months neck holding gets established and the baby is able to control movements of head but still can't prevent it from bobbing.

During these early months you and your baby are getting to know each other. The first step towards good parenting is to observe and keep track of your baby's growth and development.

Three to Six Months

- Complete head control is achieved. Turns head towards sound such as those of the bell or human voice.
- Kicks its legs vigorously and moves arms actively when lying on back.
- Rolls over from stomach to back, and back to stomach.
- Sits with support.
- Looks at hands and fingers (Hand regard).
- Tries to reach and hold objects and brings them to mouth.

- Sometimes laughs out aloud or chuckles. Makes babbling sounds.
- Recognises parents.
- Gets excited at the sight of food and starts kicking legs vigorously.
- Develops interest in surroundings.

Complete head control is usually achieved by four months of age. When a four month old baby is pulled to a sitting position from a lying down position by holding both its hands, there should be no head lag, i.e. the head should remain in line with rest of the body and not hang backwards.

While examining a five month old male baby in my clinic, I pulled him to a sitting position and found that his head was hanging completely backwards. After performing a detailed examination I told the parents that there was a definite delay in the milestones of their child and he needed further evaluation. Unfortunately, the child turned out to be a 'Mongol', and suffered from mental retardation along with heart disease. If a baby is dull, inactive and does not produce babbling sounds, it is a matter of concern and the doctor must be consulted.

Generally by the end of six months your child will be very active and show great pleasure when gently held, touched or talked to. Give your child small, safe objects to play with, such as rattles, plastic rings and keys. Play music, sing and talk to him, this stimulation is hundred times more potent than any tonic you might give him.

Six to Nine Months

- Sits without support.
- Begins to creep and crawl.
- Feeds self with a biscuit as chewing gets established.
- Transfers objects from one hand to the other.
- Makes sounds like Baba, mama.
- Knows strangers from family.
- Begins to play simple games.

Initially children allow any person to hold them, but around six months they start developing 'stranger behaviour'. Now they are happy and comfortable only with their family members and get upset if a new person comes into the house. This is a stage that children need to go through. They should be comforted and allowed to get used to different people in their own way. During this time, you can help your child if you remain calm and patient.

Between six and nine months children begin to play simple games. Parents can play peek-a-boo; clapping-hands and help children play with their toys. Expose children to many different sounds and give them musical toys, basically toys that make a lot of noise.

Nine to Twelve Months

- Pulls self to standing position and can maneouver around the house by holding on to furniture.
- Can walk with one hand held.
- Develops hand skills; picks things up with thumb and index finger.

- Deliberately throws objects on ground.
- Waves a bye-bye.
- Knows own name.
- Pays attention to simple commands such as 'No' and 'Give it to me'.
- Copies sounds such as coughing.
- Plays with family members and reciprocates affection.

This is the beginning of your child's active, exploring and discovering phase. To prevent accidents the child should be provided with a safe play area. Try to 'child proof' your home.

'Child-Proofing'—Useful tips

- Seal low placed electric points.
- Keep glass beads, coins, and pills out of reach.
- Plastic bags lying around the house are a known hazard and can cause suffocation if the child pulls the bag over his/her head.
- Keep children away while drinking hot beverages; most childhood burns occur due to accidentally spilt hot tea or coffee.
- Keep containers of insecticides and floor cleaners in safe custody. Mark them with a red X, for easy identification.
- Remove sharp edged furniture.
- Place a soft mattress on the floor.
- Cover water tank to prevent drowning.
- Always keep the main door locked, and hang a chime from it. If your little Einstein somehow, manages to open the door, the chime will keep you informed. I am

sure, you don't want a rerun of 'Baby's Day Out', with your child as the protagonist.
- Keep the first-aid kit and doctor's telephone number ready.

You can make your house safe, but don't become complacent, and never underestimate your kid's capabilities of landing into trouble—literally. At the same time provide your child with many opportunities to learn and grow. Make it fun too! Curiosity is the mother of all learning.

If at nine months the child is able to lift a small bead or a grape with index finger and thumb, it almost rules out any mental disability. Remember, children must be allowed to use the hand they prefer. Never force a left-handed child to become a right hander. This can compromise the development of hand skills because the brain will receive confusing signals.

Give your child cubes and soft rubber toys to play with. Make sure they are safe and devoid of any harmful chemicals. Show your child coloured picture books and tell him the names of animals, parts of the body and colours. You must avoid baby talk and use simple words and short sentences. Provide lots of love and attention and always respond to the affection shown by your child.

Twelve to Fifteen Months
- Walks alone and creeps upstairs.
- Can build a tower two cubes.
- Draws a line with crayons.
- Starts using a spoon but rotates it near the mouth.

- Lifts cup with two hands and drinks.
- Starts speaking in jargon with some intelligible words.
- Plays simple ball games, rolls the ball to the other person.
- Understands more of what is being told.

Child proofing the house is still required. Watch your child and try to prevent falls and injuries. Walk hand-in-hand and play ball with your child. To develop hand skills give cubes and plastic cups to stack. Let the child drink milk from a cup and use a spoon to feed self. Sit back patiently and remain calm; your little one is bound to be messy at first.

Around fifteen months children start experimenting with language; they speak unintelligible words, with the voice going up and down as if speaking (jargoning). To outsiders this appears absurd and funny, but parents may comprehend what the child is trying to communicate. Teach your child the 'should' and 'should not', but give only one simple instruction at a time.

Fifteen to Eighteen Months

- Starts to run. Pulls wheeled toys.
- Seats self on a small chair.
- Makes a tower of three cubes.
- Imitates scribbling and vertical strokes.
- Turns two or three pages of a book at a time.
- Repeats simple words, may have a vocabulary of 5-10 words.
- Identifies one or more parts of body.
- Indicates wet pants.

- Domestic mimicry: imitates simple actions such as reading, sweeping the floor or washing utensils.

Your 'little shadow' is now with you all the time, and like a true shadow, imitates your actions. He picks up a book, a broom, or a utensil just like you. He washes clothes, waters plants, sweeps the floor and generally helps you around the house. You must 'tolerate' being helped even if this inevitably slows you down. Your little one is learning by imitating you.

You and your child can now become good friends. Colour with your child, read stories and point to familiar objects. Always listen and pay attention to your child. A child who indicates wet pants must be praised, this reinforces the pattern.

Eighteen to Twenty-four Months
- Goes up and down the stairs two feet per step.
- Builds a tower of six cubes.
- Turns one page of a book at a time.
- Can combine two different words such as 'want biscuit', 'play ball'.
- Takes off shoes and socks.
- Knows self in mirror or picture. Uses words such as 'I', 'Me', and 'Your'.
- Likes to move to music.
- Will play next to, but not with other children.
- May show some interest in using the toilet. Remains dry in the day.

Your 'bundle of joy' has now become a 'bundle of boundless energy' and coping with it will surely make you 'breathless'. Your little one will keep coming back with more and still more questions. Reply you must, even if you are at your wit's end. Apparently simple but perplexing queries of your child will stretch your imagination to its limits. Patience and understanding should keep you afloat. Remember you are your child's first teacher; don't let this opportunity go unutilised.

Allow your child to make choices whenever possible; for example ask, "Do you want a green candy or a red one?" Play music for your child and help with simple dance like movements. Keep interacting constantly; ask the names of toys and household objects, tell the names of animals, fruits and flowers. Don't punish your child for any toilet accidents. These are early days; gradually the child will have better control.

Twenty-four to Thirty-six Months

- Jumps, kicks a ball.
- Likes to ride a tricycle.
- Goes upstairs one foot per step but comes down two feet per step.
- Builds a tower of nine cubes.
- Imitates a cross and circle.
- Knows full name, age, and sex.
- Repeats numbers and rhymes.
- Often says 'No' to bedtime, certain foods and simple requests.

- Helps in dressing and undressing. Puts on shoes (not laces).
- Plays with other children; may share toys.
- Uses toilet more often. Remains dry in the night.

Take your child on walk or to a park and help him in climbing and sliding. Allow the child to play and run barefoot sometimes. Let your child use paints, clay and crayons. Give blocks to build and simple puzzles to solve.

Teach your child to feed self, to dress and to use the toilet. All children love to play with water; let them have their fun. Make sure child gets to play with other children.

We all know about 'The Terrible Teens', but have you heard about 'The Terrible Twos'? The little chap offers a standard no to bedtime, food and other simple requests of yours. During this stage children have very definite opinions about things and may often disagree with you. This is very common so don't get flustered. They are not trying to be grumpy or rude; they need to learn that their feelings count and that they are also an important part of the family.

Three to four Years

- Goes down stairs one foot per step. Has good balance.
- Catches a large ball.
- Copies a square and capital letters.
- Draws a man with four body parts.
- Can count from 1-10.
- Names longer of the two lines.
- Exhibits self-help skills; washes and dries self, brushes teeth.

- Plays with several children.
- Goes to toilet alone.
- Tells stories.

Your child's brain is maturing very rapidly and is flooded with ideas and questions. In the rush to tell you about everything, the child may stumble over words. Don't get worried, this again is very common.

Delay in speech development is diagnosed only if the child does not show signs of meaningful speech by the age of four years. Girls speak earlier than boys. Tongue-tie should never be considered as a cause for delayed speech, though at times, it might be responsible for difficulty in pronouncing certain syllables.

Don't get anxious if you find your child lagging behind in some specific area as compared to other children. At this stage, children are going through rapid changes and a skill that may not be there during one month may appear the next month.

All children like playing Hide-and-seek, but they won't mind solving riddles either; for example ask your child "what is round, yellow and comes out in the day?" While playing with your child try to develop the concepts of large/small, long/short, near/far and on/off.

To develop hand skills, let your child cut pictures from old magazines and newspapers. Take your child to different places such as a library, an aquarium or a Zoo. There is no substitute for on-the-spot learning. Encourage your child to ask questions and try to give truthful answers.

Four to five Years

- Skips, hops, swings, climbs.
- Draws a triangle.
- Dresses self completely, ties shoe laces, combs hair.
- Uses full sentences and tells longer stories.
- Shows understanding of-tomorrow, yesterday, next year.
- Knows about money, appliances.
- While playing games with other children can agree to rules.
- Likes to sing, dance and act.
- Is interested in physical difference between boys and girls.
- Shows more independence and may visit a neighbour unescorted.

To function independently the child should feel confident about self. Allow your child to choose clothes, give simple household chores and show interest in what your child has to say to you. Your child is now more interested in playing with other children, but will require your help in learning how to get along with others and to give-and-take. Tell your child as much about the world as you can simply and honestly.

The developmental milestones described above constitute broad guidelines only and variation is a rule rather than an exception. Children develop in their own ways and different children may achieve the same milestone at different ages. Some children are better at climbing and jumping; others are better at drawing and music. Your child may not be athletically inclined but may be very good at solving puzzles and mathematical problems.

It is not possible to make a reliable diagnosis of developmental retardation unless an infant is closely watched, observed and examined till the age of six months. In general, rapid development, especially social, adaptive and linguistic, during childhood is associated with superior intelligence in later life. However, it is difficult to reliably predict the future personality of a child on the basis of psychosocial characteristics during infancy.

Finally, if you find that your little shadow is no longer by your side; you have succeeded in your initial endeavour. Congratulations! Your child has taken the first steps into the vast world of opportunity.

Facts for Parents

- Most newborn babies lose weight during the first few days, but subsequently start gaining weight and regain their birth weight by the age of seven days.
- During the first year of its life, a baby triples its birth weight, i.e. a newborn weighing 3 kg should weigh 9 kg at one year. This never happens again in life, so don't miss out on this unique opportunity.
- During first year of life, average daily weight gain is 30 grams in first quarter, 20 grams in second quarter and 10 grams in third quarter. If your child gains 900 grams per month during the first four months, you should be happy, but even if the weight gain is only 300 grams

per month from 9th to 12th month: you should not be worried.
- Between 4 to 12 years average weight gain is about 2 kg per year. Most mothers are unduly and unnecessarily worried about the appetite and weight gain of children during this phase.
- A child measures approximately 50 cm at birth. Height increases by 25 cm in first year, 12.5 cm during second year, 7.5-10 cm in third year and subsequently it varies between 5.0-7.5 cm per year, till the growth spurt of puberty occurs.
- It is possible to predict ultimate adult height of children with an error of plus/minus 4 cm. Tanner has suggested that anticipated adult height is approximately double of height at 2 years or 1.87 times of height at 3 years.

2

From Nobody to Somebody

Every child born into the world is a new thought of God, and ever-fresh and radiant possibility.
—Kate Douglas Wiggin

With the acquisition of hand and body coordination, linguistic capabilities and social skills, the basic infrastructure needed for personality development of a child is ready. The personality of a child is the final outcome of a complex interplay of three main determinants—

- Heredity
- Environment
- Self Concept

Heredity

Let us reminisce about your 'bundle of joy' and those early blissful days. You were ecstatic, and every thing seemed nice and beautiful. Then one late night your little one suddenly decided to wake you up and give you your first test of parenthood. It cried nonstop, didn't want milk and was not wet either. Well! You took your baby in your lap, the crying stopped and two little eyes focussed on your face. The moment you tried to put it down it started shrieking again.

When this getting up, crying and remaining awake for long hours during the night repeated itself on a regular basis, you started getting worried. Is the little one all right? Can it be 'colic' or 'gas' that is disturbing the sleep? Is my baby developing normally?

You rushed to your doctor; your mind in a turmoil. After a brief examination and with a broad smile the doctor declared that your baby is in pink of health. He told you: "Actually the little fellow does not want to sleep in the night. Your baby's sleep rhythm—the normal pattern of sleeping in the night and remaining awake during the day—is not yet established".

You then ran up a long list of your friends whose babies—ever since they were born—always slept like a log during the night. Why doesn't your child follow the same pattern? The answer to this question is: even very young babies reveal differences not only in their behaviour— sleep pattern, feeding habits but also in their reactions to a particular kind of stimuli. Some of them are startled at even slight sounds or cry if sunlight hits their faces; others are seemingly insensitive to such stimulation. Thus conditions that one baby can tolerate may be quite upsetting to another.

These subtle differences in responses and behaviour patterns indicate that different personality traits are present in the babies right form the time of birth itself and are a manifestation of their different genetic endowment. At conception when, the ovum of the female is fertilised by the sperm of the male—each new human being receives a genetic inheritance which influences the development of some traits more than others. Although this influence is most noticeable in physical features such as: colour of the eyes and hair, shape of nose, build and complexion, it also appears to play an influential role in reaction tendencies and sensitivity to various situations. This tendency to react differently to similar stimuli is carried forward from infancy to young adulthood.

Environment

The basic personality inherited by the child is greatly influenced by the environment in which he or she lives. A child's genetic inheritance interacts with and is shaped by the environmental factors operative in his or her world. This interaction results in the emergence of a self-image or the personality of the child. Self-image is responsible for directing further development and behaviour of the child.

A child is exposed to various interactions with other people, typically beginning with family members and going on to include the peer group members. Other important people who are in constant close contact with the child also influence the process of personality development of the child. Much of a child's personality reflects experiences with these key persons. The child who is rejected and mistreated is likely to develop quite differently from one who is encouraged and loved.

Why are some children reserved and shy, and others open and loving? Why do some run away from their homes, while others are adjusted to their home situation? Answers to these and several such questions can be found in the child's environment. The behaviour patterns children learn depend heavily on models to which they are exposed. The socio-cultural environment is the source of differences as well as similarities in personality development.

Prateek, seven, can pluck the strings of a Guitar and can hum a song or two. It's the influence of his neighborhood, where a music teacher conducts music classes. **Raunak**, five, is quite adept at cursing and some of his uttering can put goons to shame. He didn't have to take tuition for learning these invectives, a drunkard father provided him with free tutorials.

It's an undisputed fact of life: we can't escape our socio-cultural milieu. Our genetic endowment provides our potentialities for development, but the shaping of this potential—in terms of perceiving, thinking, feeling and acting-depends heavily on the inputs we receive from our physical and socio-cultural environment.

Environment leaves its imprints even on the faces of rocks, can a delicate human brain escape its vagaries!

Self-concept

In addition to heredity and environment, there is a third very important factor which determines the final outcome of the process of personality development: the concept of 'self'. So far as is known, children are not born with any particular self-concept but as they grow the concept of 'me', 'I' or 'self' is gradually established. The child starts using statements like 'I know', 'I want' and 'I will'.

A child views the things as he or she thinks they really are. These are known as reality assumptions, and are an important part of personality development. Several questions start cropping up in child's mind:
- What kind of person I am? Am I good or bad?
- Is the surrounding world favourable or against me? E.g. If Varun is my friend, why did he hit me? Why did the teacher scold me? Doesn't she like me?

These, apparently simple questions can lead to extreme confusion, if the child doesn't receive appropriate and positive inputs at home and in school. Parents and teachers should try to explain things in their proper perspective; a child's question must never be left unanswered.

Gradually the child starts exploring the possibility of changing or modifying things for his/her own benefit. Improving personal standing amongst peers, as well as seniors, becomes important to the child. A need to impress people is felt by all children at some stage of personality development. These actions of the child are essential for personal growth and social progress.

Still later the child starts attaching values to actions, objects and people. The concept of right and wrong, good or bad, desirable and undesirable starts developing. This is the final step, which ultimately guides a child's behavior. The development of correct values may prevent the child from stealing or behaving in other ways that he/she considers unethical. Such a child feels secure and has feelings of adequacy, competence and worth. The reverse is also very much true, and the child who faces rejection and ridicule grows up with a poor self-image.

Finally as the child develops a sense of selfhood, he or she starts behaving in accordance with the norms as perceived and established by the society. Thus, in addition to heredity and environment, the concept of 'Self' also plays an important role in the process of personality development.

Crucial needs for personality development

All children have certain essential emotional needs. These needs are inherent to all human beings and are as important for positive personality development, as nutrition is for healthy physical growth. Let us examine what these needs are and how they affect the personality of a child.

1. *Curiosity*

All of us are born with a factory-fitted, inquisitive mind, which strives to understand and achieve a meaningful picture of the world around it. Curiosity is an in-built quality of the human brain that drives the 'Search-engine' of human knowledge. Young children are naturally extremely curious about everything; for them most things hold novelty. Mastering an activity, gaining control over a situation, all are a source of immense pleasure and satisfaction for the child.

I am sure the first place your daughter or son poked a finger at was an electric point. Before you realise it your child is adept at using a TV remote, or has turned into an expert disk jockey- the home grown DJ who never fails to find the right song. Isn't it strange? The little fellow can't yet tie the shoelaces, but can accomplish such tasks with consummate ease. Human brain is capricious by nature; enjoyable tasks are learnt at great speed, but uninteresting things make it move like a snail. This holds good for the adult as well as the child.

Your child's questions may appear trivial to you (I won't advocate using the word stupid), but their answers are very important for the child. Through such probing he is able to unravel the mysteries of the world.

2. *Security*

The need for security remains with us all our lives. Children are more prone to developing feelings of insecurity because they are not yet familiar with the depravity of the world. Not knowing how to deal with a problem can upset a child. Repeated exposures to unknown and apparently threatening situations may end in acute anxiety.

Saumya, four, was brought to my clinic for a typhoid shot. On seeing her dread, I promised her a chocolate and a rubber if she didn't cry. I was amazed by her response: "I will not cry otherwise the ghost will kill me. Please give the chocolate and rubber to the ghost, so that he doesn't come after me."

Saumya's father, a Sales Officer, was mostly out of town. Her mother worked in a private company and was out of the house for long hours. In their absence Saumya's elder brother and sister were terrorising her with tales of ghosts living in the vicinity of their home. The absence of parental care and assurance was responsible for Saumya's plight.

Lack of parental interaction invariably leads to development of feelings of insecurity in the child. Insecurity can also arise if the child has to cope with a dominating and demoralising peer group. Pervasive and chronic feelings of insecurity typically lead to apprehension and failure to participate fully in one's world.

3. *Adequacy and Competence*

Adequacy and competence are closely related and are the hallmarks of a child who feels secure. Every child needs to feel capable of dealing with day to day challenges. Parents have to be sagacious in encouraging their children to face new challenges. This is especially important because initial setbacks can 'set back' a child by quite a few steps. The early playful and investigative behaviour of children must be encouraged. This behaviour involves a process of "reality testing" and is ultimately responsible for learning, reasoning and other coping abilities, which are greatly expanded by formal education.

Gauri, six, used to observe her father make several copies of a letter, using carbon paper. For her birthday party, she wrote out invitations to her friends by putting old used carbons between the pages of an invitation pad. Her parents were pleasantly surprised and recounted the incident to all present on her birthday. It is not difficult to imagine Gauri's feeling of adequacy and competence. This praise, probably, was the most precious present she received on her birthday.

Parents have a very important role to play if they want their children to develop faith in their capabilities, and acquire competence to achieve their goals.

4. *Love and Belonging*

A baby is born with a need to be loved and never outgrows it. A sense of belonging is crucial to healthy personality development and successful adjustments in life. Love and warmth imparted by the parents to their child remain the most important determinants for developing an assured outlook towards life.

Love and a sense of belonging can make a child overcome several adverse circumstances, such as a physical handicap, poverty etc. Affection and acceptance act as cushions against disappointment and as shields against antagonism. The best available balm for 'hurt-feelings' and 'bruised-egos' is the warmth exuding from the parents.

The need for close ties remains throughout life but becomes especially important in times of stress or crisis e.g. during examination or at the time of a stage performance. Failing an interview is a crisis, which can be overcome easily if the parent are forthcoming with their love and support.

5. *Approval and Self-esteem (Worth)*

Approval of accomplishments is a need, which must be fulfilled for further achievement. Appreciation for building a tower of three cubes encourages the child to add the fourth and the fifth cube. Praise for good manners, neat writing, keeping the room clean, acts as a positive reinforcement and leads to establishment of desired behaviour.

Self-esteem has its early foundation in parental affirmation of worth and in mastery of early developmental tasks. When your child learns to draw a circle don't dismiss it as being trivial. Your approval and guidance can make the child convert that circle into a human face, by adding eyes, nose and mouth to it. As the child crosses new milestones and receives encouragement for them, his or her self-esteem gets a further boost.

A child requires both, approval of the parents as well as of the society. This fulfills the need to feel good about oneself and worthy of the respect of others. Achievements in areas considered important: academics, sports, dramatics, music help the child grow in confidence and develop a positive self-image.

6. *Identity*

Once the child has a positive self-image and a sense of

worth, the search for self-identity becomes easy. Initially parents serve as an alter ego of the child, but later the need to identify with peer groups and young adults is felt. As the child enters into adolescence, there is an overwhelming dependence on the values and standards of prominent peer-group members. The child tries to become an integral part of the group and derives important learning experiences from it. Finding an important role in the group through active participation helps the child to develop confidence and leadership qualities.

In the beginning this may cause resentment at home. But unless the child is in bad company, it is not damaging to the personality development.

7. *Values*

A child without values develops into a clueless adult. Values, as approved and accepted by the society must be instilled and reinforced repeatedly by the parents. The best way to raise a morally strong child is to be a moral person yourself. If you're honest and truthful, decent and caring, your children would be the same. If you lie, cheat or curse, even if occasionally, you are sending wrong signals to your child. When a child is unable to find uniform value patterns, confusion sets in, and the unlimited energies of childhood remain unutilised. A satisfactory value pattern leads to development of competencies, positive self-image and a confident personality.

Are you a moral parent?

1. Before travelling by 'train' do you 'train' your children

to drop a year or two from their ages to avail 50% discount?
2. When you go to places with free entry for babies, do you take your school going child in your arms?
3. When a motorist overtakes you from the wrong side, do you curse him with choicest invectives, using meaningful hand gestures?
4. Do you jump red lights, park illegally and enter one way streets from the wrong side, if the traffic-policemen is not watching?
5. You have planned a trip to a hill station or there is a marriage in the family, and your child will miss school. Do you make a distant relative drop dead or arrange a false medical certificate for your child?
6. You see your child cheating in a quiz competition, do you reprimand the child later or overlook the fact especially if he/she wins?

The End Product

Personality development is a complex process which involves innumerable inputs (stimuli) and outputs (responses). The end products of this process are—development of independence, self-control and competence.

Development of Independence

The developing foetus in the mother's womb is entirely dependent upon her for all its needs; placenta being its lifeline literally as well as practically. After birth, the infant again remains largely dependent upon the mother for most of its needs, but gradually starts showing maturity in responses.

From initial cooing sounds to recitation of nursery rhymes, your little one traverses a long winding path. The early hesitant steps metamorphose into feet that can run and dance. With pride you observe your child using a spoon deftly, or drinking milk holding the cup in his/her little hands. From tricycle to a bicycle, from mere jumping to rope skipping, from bathtub to the swimming pool, your child makes steady progress.

The total dependence becomes a thing of past as the adolescent and then the young adult becomes totally independent. Along with this growth towards independence and self-direction there is the development of a clear sense of personal identity. Acquisition of information, self-control, competencies and values accompanies the development of independence. Family and society play an important role in this growth.

Acquisition of Self Control

Other than physical size, what is the one most distinctive feature that separates a child from an adult? It is the ability of the grown-ups to control and modify behaviour according to the need and requirement of the situation. Ask a little boy to part with his favourite toy or a bar of chocolate; a 'no' is all you will get.

As he or she grows up, the child gets several opportunities to perceive and face reality. This involves distinguishing between fantasy and reality, controlling impulse and desire, and learning to cope with the inevitable frustrations of life. As the child is able to exercise control over self, he or she becomes more effective and efficient in confirming to the behavioural norms set by the family and the society.

Development of competence

In medical jargon:

- Infant is a child upto one-year of age.
- Toddler is a child upto three years of age.
- Pre-school child is a child between three to five years.
- School going child is a child beyond five years.
- Teenager..... is a teenager!

The entire pre-adult period is directed towards the acquisition of intellectual, emotional, social skills, which come in good use in adulthood. The child gradually learns to exercise control over emotions and can direct the flow of emotions for enrichment of the quality of life.

Thus, the incompetencies are shed and a competent, self-assured personality is acquired. But this might not always be the case, and the development of personality may be abnormal or faulty depending on the quality and interaction of genetic and environmental factors. If emotional deprivation (rejection, disapproval, insecurity, inadequacy) takes place, personality disorders and maladaptive behaviour results.

It has been observed that by the age of four most children have a fairly clear picture of themselves and their world. They become capable of discriminating, interpreting and evaluating experiences, challenges and situations. Your child now becomes capable of cognition i.e. the notions of perceiving, knowing and conceiving and from being nobody the child becomes somebody. It follows that the early period of a child's life should be made maximally conducive for the development of a positive personality.

Herbert Hoover said, "Children are our most natural resource." Let us follow his advice and try to turn this vast resource into an infinite treasure.

3

The Struggles of Childhood

"Seldom do we think of the child as a small human being, carrying on his own struggle to make sense out of life, to meet his own needs, to master the challenges presented by life—but differing from adults especially in the proportion of newness to which he is exposed."
—Murphy

Growing-up is a stressful situation. With growth, as newer capabilities, both in terms of physical strength and mental activity, are acquired, the child starts experimenting with new stimuli. New toys, new friends, new sounds, new sights; there is a whole new world in front of the child to explore. To the inexperienced child each new situation is the harbinger of a fresh challenge. Inherent and acquired competencies help the child to overcome some of these but failures do happen and are an essential part of growing up. Perception of shortcomings and deficiencies inevitably leads to hurt and anxiety. This happens to all of us, but adults have experience on their side, which helps them to overcome the adverse circumstances with comparative ease.

Children develop certain behaviours or responses by which they are able to soften the impact of failure. These behaviours help in alleviating anxiety and hurt, and in the process protect the child's feelings of adequacy and worth. The idea behind discussing these responses or behaviours is to make the parents aware of their true significance.

If you find your child manifesting these tendencies, be careful, considerate and supportive. Your child needs your help desperately! Your lack of understanding will only increase the desperation and may even scar permanently the child's personality.

Let us examine some important behavioural patterns by which children protect and preserve their self-esteem.

Refusal

Refusing or denying a reality is probably the most basic of all responses used to preserve feelings of worth. In this an attempt is made to 'screen out' or 'obliterate' unfavourable realities by either ignoring them or by refusing to acknowledge them.

A child may refuse to discuss unpleasant topics, like a poor performance in an examination or a complaint made by teacher for some mischief. Denial provides a temporary succour, and gives insulation from the full impact of a traumatic situation.

Constructing An Unreal World

Children who get repeated rebuffs or face successive failures may become frustrated and recalcitrant. To overcome the associated feelings of inadequacy and incompetence they start living in a world of fantasy. This world is marked by the achievement of desired goals. These children may picture themselves as famous film stars or celebrated athletes or as exceptionally brilliant students. These fantasies act as "Safety valves" and allow the release of pent-up anger and frustration. They provide relief from humiliation and hurt and protect the child's self-esteem. This type of fantasising is called the conquering hero pattern.

Continued parental apathy can lead to the development of unwanted habits and the child falling prey to delinquent gangs. **Aniket** repeatedly failed to score runs in inter-school cricket matches. He was removed from the school team. His ego hurt, the child started fantasising himself to be the famous cricketing icon: Sachin Tendulkar. He would fantasise hitting sixes and fours of every ball and scoring centuries at will. He even purchased stylish black sunglasses to look like Sachin and pestered his father to buy him a complete cricket gear.

Each evening, Aniket would carry his cricket kit on his bicycle to the school play-ground, and hang around with other boys. He returned home late in the evenings with tales of his explosive batting and how every one called him the "master blaster".

His parents remained unaware of the 'ground-reality'—till the day Aniket's father happened to visit the school playground. He got the shock of his life. Aniket was sitting on the boundary wall with some boys and smoking. His father brought him back home and checked his cricket kit—it was practically empty. Aniket had sold off his cricketing gear for some easy money.

Don't let this happen to your child. It happened to Aniket because his parents did not keep track of his activities. So they did not realise that their child had suffered failure and was living in a world of fantasy. The message is clear: involve yourself with your child. **Success deserves a hug but failure needs an even tighter embrace.**

There is another pattern of fantasising known as the suffering hero pattern. Here the children start believing that their failure occur because they are suffering from some dangerous disease, debilitating handicap, quirk of fate or a curse of some evil spirit. These children do not admit personal incompetencies or inadequacies. On the contrary they believe that when their parents, teachers and others come to know about their difficulties and realise the courage it took to overcome them, they will be sympathetic and admiring.

In this manner explanations for poor performance or failure are provided and feelings of adequacy and worth are preserved. These children need opportunities to succeed, which must be created by the teachers and parents. Success will allow them to step out of the world of fantasy and find a niche for themselves in the world of reality.

Forgetting the Unpleasant

Young children are bound to come across several unpleasant or threatening situations. These can generate feelings of insecurity and may undermine a child's self-image. Such events are deliberately removed from consciousness. (e.g. failing an examination, punishment by teachers or loss in a game). This is also called 'selective forgetting', because children easily retain the pleasant and happy events in their consciousness. Getting a monitor's badge or a "good" in the note-book will not be forgotten and the child will immediately show these to the parents. The repression of the unpleasant and reproduction of the pleasant is needed to preserve the feeling of worth and should be considered as instinctive attempts of the child to prevent self-devaluation.

Finding Motives

When children behave badly, i.e. in a manner contrary to the values instilled by parents and norms ascribed by the society, they try to find plausible explanations and rationalise their faulty behaviour.

Sonika spent the money given to her for buying a compass box on an ice cream soda. After returning home she was a bit tense and perturbed, but became her normal self later in the day. She had been able to justify to herself that she had not eaten an ice cream soda for a month, so there was nothing wrong in having one. Moreover she knew that since ice cream soda was costly, on the next visit to an ice cream parlour her parents would buy her a vanilla cup.

The process of justification also aids in softening the disappointment associated with unattainable goals. Children may justify their poor performance in examinations by reasoning that they are refusing to get involved in the competition or that they are not bothered about the ranks. Thus by deciding that the goal is not worth much–they try to preserve their worth and self esteem in their own eyes and believe that others are also naïve enough to think so. Some may even rationalise their mediocre performance by saying that, they did not try hard enough and if and when they decide they will pass the examinations with flying colours.

Parents can easily recognise a child who is hunting for motive and plausible explanations for maladaptive behaviour or failure to achieve goals.

- The key is to keep communication lines with the child. There will be several inconsistencies or contradictions in his answers. These would be plainly obvious to parents but the child will not be able to recognise them.
- On seeing parental disbelief the child will hunt for fresh reasons and justifications.
- When the reason or explanations are questioned; the child becomes upset. Such questioning is a threat to the defenses the child has managed to raise against self devaluation.

These children are putting up a brave front for their shortcomings and are extremely vulnerable. While approaching such children, parents have to be supportive as well as tactful. A child who presents a smug exterior even after scoring poor marks should not be run down. Showing the mark sheets of previous examinations where he or she had performed better will help in rebuilding confidence and self-image.

Blaming Others

The student who fails an examination will blame the teachers for being unfair and prejudiced, the runaway teenager will blame the parents for not being understanding and loving enough, and the small boy punished for fighting may protest: "It wasn't my fault-he hit me first". Even inanimate objects are not spared and a four-year old, who falls down from a baby-chair, can attack it with blows and kicks. A child, who gets into the habit of blaming others for his own failure, may eventually blame fate and misfortune when no other object can be found.

I remember a funny graffiti: "Its not whether you win or lose, but where you put the blame". Thus when a batsman gets bowled he blames the pitch, when a footballer misses a goal he curses his shoe and the cue comes to the rescue of a billiards player who misses a simple cannon. Human race is extremely adept at passing the buck. It seems 'blaming others' is a basic metabolic process of human brain.

Loner Child

Situations, which are viewed as disappointing are avoided; peers with whom there have been hurtful experiences are shunned. Gradually the child reduces emotional interactions as a safeguard against further devaluation. Thus an exuberant, outgoing and carefree child turns into a recluse.

Sheena was not good at singing and dancing, so to hide her inadequacies she avoided going to the parties where these were going to figure prominently.

Avneesh was quiz masters' delight, and loved to go to birthday parties where quizzing was a popular activity. Suddenly he started avoiding parties and lost interest in quizzing. Gentle probing by his parents revealed that Amandeep the 'big bully' was the reason why Avneesh had stopped going to the parties.

In case of Sheena emotional insulation provided a protective shell against the disappointment of not being as accomplished as her peers. Avoiding parties saved Avneesh from emotional hurt and possible physical injury.

While this phenomenon, initially at least, helps the child to preserve self-esteem, it removes opportunities of learning new skills and may finally foster feelings of inferiority. The child is deprived of participation in activities of life—so important for development of competence and confidence.

Redeeming or Atonement

We all believe that through apology or punishment we are absolved of our sins. Life must go on, and for further progress and future achievements a child has to be given a second chance.

Let us continue with the example of Aniket, who was

caught smoking by his father, near the school playground. After reaching home Aniket apologised repeatedly, but his father was so upset and angry that he gave him a severe thrashing. Initially Aniket was in a pitiable state of mind, but gradually he started to feel that after being punished for his wrong behaviour his misdeed had been negated and he could now start all over again with renewed parental approval.

This is an important line of thought and is essential for avoiding self-devaluation. Parents cannot hang the child for every sin and they have to allow him to make a fresh beginning. After some days Aniket's father brought him a new cricket kit and took him for cricket coaching. Today Aniket is back in the school team, scoring boundaries by the dozen, not merely fantasising about them.

Regression

When a new addition to the family, in the form of a baby girl, seemingly undermined his status **Sankalp** reverted to bed-wetting and other infantile behaviour that had once brought him parental attention. The developmental process from dependence to independence (or from being nobody to somebody) is by no means an easy one. Consequently, it is not surprising that in the face of a new perceived threat Sankalp regressed to infantile behaviour. For in regression the child retreats from reality to a less demanding personal status-one that involves lowered aspirations and more easily accomplished feats. This is done to gain attention as well as to avoid losing faith in one's own capabilities.

Compensation

Children can develop feelings of inferiority and inadequacy due to real or imagined personal defects or weaknesses. To neutralise these feelings and preserve self-esteem they manifest certain compensatory reactions.

A physically unattractive girl may develop an exceptionally pleasing personality. She is helpful and considerate, and tries to become a favourite of younger children to compensate for the indifference of peers. A puny boy may turn from athletics to scholarly pursuits. The child, who was dropped from the local football team, forms a team of other such children and becomes its captain.

Many compensatory reactions are undesirable and can hamper proper development of a child. Some children who feel insecure may try to show-off to grab attention. They may brag about their relatives, real or imaginary, and their palatial bungalows and luxurious cars. Some children exaggerate their own accomplishments; their percentage of marks keeps jumping higher and higher each time they open their mouths. Some may try to criticise others in attempts to cut them down to their own size.

The struggles, the contests, the rivalries, the contentions, the sparring and the skirmishes of childhood are all there to see and observe. I suppose they are a must if the child has to join the battle and survive in today's turbulent, stressful times. I believe that these manoeuvers prepare the child for the cut-throat competition that is just round the corner.

4

Home: The Base Camp

There are only two lasting bequests we can hope to give our children. One of these is roots; the other, wings.

—Hoddine Cater

Homes are building blocks of the edifice of our society. Home influences outweigh the effects of all other environmental factors combined together, in shaping a child's personality. Psychologists believe that most of the emotional conflicts, maladaptive behaviours and failures in life can be traced back to early traumatic experiences at home.

In view of this, the role of parents in shaping the destiny of a child cannot be overestimated (and must never be underestimated). Most children who grow into successful adults come from homes where parental attitudes are favourable and where a wholesome relationship exists between them and their parents. Children sharing a warm and stable relationship with their parents are friendly, tolerant, constructive and affectionate. They are successful socially and possess good intellectual skills. On the other hand, those who come from homes with unfavourable parent-child interactions tend to be intolerant of others, impulsive, socially withdrawn and have poor intellectual skills. Thus, parenting is probably the most important element in the process of growth of confidence, nurturing of self-esteem and ultimate success in life.

No two homes are exactly alike and this reflects in the varied and unpredictable child rearing practices adopted by the parents. Traditions and personal prejudices can affect a child's psychological development. Faulty parental attitudes like overprotection, indulgence or rejection have adverse effects on the child's personality development. On the other hand, democratic guidance by parents helps the child's personality development.

For the average parent bringing up a child is fraught with self-doubt, insecurity and emotional stress, but few parents will ever doubt their ability to rear children. Inspite of best parental efforts some children respond and behave idiosyncratically. Parents of such children need to be more assertive, but at the same time they have to be more supportive of the critical developmental needs of these children and it is a pleasant feeling to know that somehow most parents manage to do so.

The Ideal Home

Is there an entity like this? Perhaps yes, but undoubtedly it is an infrequent phenomenon. A home which is safe, secure and full of genuine love and care, is the ideal 'nurturing place' for the fragile 'psychological' software loaded in the human brain. It is this software that runs and controls all human actions and reactions.

A child's personality is largely derived from the initial parent-child interactions at home. Parents serve as models for their children and influence them by their actions and what they do on a given occasion. Parents who are calm and soothing and generally remain unruffled in day to day crises are 'ideal parents'. These parents provide a safe world or a belief that there is a solution to every problem. Their children are likely to be confident and self-assured while facing any exigency. Parents, who get upset and irritated by problems, give negative feedback to their children. These children thus do not learn to remain calm in the face of a crisis.

Homes where children feel connected to their parents, foster a sence of belonging. Parents should allow children to help them in household chores, even if this inevitably slows down the speed of work. Parental disinterest and detachment makes the child feel isolated and lonely. Such children may start feeling rejected and can develop feelings of insecurity and worthlessness.

Parents who show genuine pride and delight in their child's achievements, however insignificant (riding a tricycle, skipping rope, tying shoe-laces–anything), give positive feedback to the child. This motivates him or her to achieve further goals and form a positive self-image. Similarly an affectionate hug for good conduct or, a gentle reprimand for a misdeed, not only influences the child's behaviour at that point of time but also modifies it on future similar occasions. Judicious use of the words 'good' and 'bad' is much more effective in moulding behaviour of the child than either emotional outburst or physical punishment.

Parents must encourage children to ask questions and should promote 'information exchange'. This is essential for healthy personality development and the best way to know the world. An ideal family tends to show a much higher incidence of supportive interactions and communication.

A significant change seen over the last few years is that children are increasingly being treated as equals by the parents. It is an undisputed fact that children want to do things the way the 'grown-ups' do. When children are treated as 'little ones', they continue to be immature. When they are treated as equals, in adult-like fashion, they mature earlier, and develop a sense of responsibility. They look upon themselves as 'grown-ups', behave like 'grown-ups' and have a positive 'self-image'. When their questions are answered by their parents in a serious and earnest manner they develop self-respect and feel worthy of their parents' love and affection.

A home with well-adjusted and compatible parents provides the child with the ideal launch pad. Parental quarreling, conflict and general tension are unfortunate conditions for growing children, representing a threat to their 'base of operations', and the only security they know. A harmonious parental relationship acts as a conduit for greater parent-child harmony. True concern and compassion for the interests of the child sustains and further augments emotional bonding between parents and the child.

Sociability of the parents, i.e. their status in the society, the respect they command from friends and colleagues, all contribute towards positive personality development in the child. Active home environment, with intense and warm interactions between inmates as well as with outsiders, stimulates the socialisation process of the child. These homes produce young people who are confident, successful and well adjusted in the society.

A judicious mix of competition and co-operation among siblings is essential for optimal personality development. Healthy rivalry is in fact desirable, as it prepares for future battles. Parents can use it for motivating the child with lesser achievement, but they must avoid undue comparisons.

Adjustments and understanding between siblings gradually results in emotional bonding. They learn the art of sharing and caring early. I recall my elder daughter Misha getting a nasty cut while playing. Zoya not even four then, promptly fetched a band-aid and a Barbie doll. I was thrilled and overwhelmed that the small child could come up with such a thoughtful gesture. I feel that the greatest asset one can possess in life is a caring and affectionate brother or sister.

Case Study

Astha Sarin, thirteen, is the eldest of three children in the Sarin family. She has a younger brother aged ten and a sister aged eight. She is secure, serene and well adjusted both at home and in school. She tends to be dominant sometimes towards her siblings, but is very popular with her classmates, who admire her talents for leadership and organisation.

Astha's home represents a delectable combination of many factors productive of a congenial environment of positive personality development in a child. Her parents themselves are well adjusted, outgoing and sociable. They enjoy the company of their children and treat them as individuals. They are capable of appraising their children objectively in a detached manner, at the same time they exude warmth and devotion towards them without hesitation or awkwardness. Every child gets due importance and is treated as a full member of the family.

Mrs. Sarin is a computer professional who operates from her home and does regular work for various firms. She is stable, kindly, good humoured and possesses remarkable patience. Her keen sense of humour enlivens even the dullest moments, making her family a cheerful lot.

Mr. Sarin is a Senior Executive who inspite of his busy schedule never fails to involve himself in the day to day running of the household. Dinner-time is discussion time, where each member of the 'family council' is present and participates actively in the dialogue. After dinner coffee for the parents and milk for children is a tradition strictly adhered to! These hot beverages are taken in the living room, where discussions may heat up or end in laughter, with plenty of 'leg pulling' without the intention of toppling anyone.

It should be emphasized that Sarins' home is not without its routine problems. Mrs. Sarin has to contend with the usual disciplinary crisis, sibling rivalries, food prejudices and preferences and general reversals faced by most mothers. But because of her more than average tolerance and patience she manages these situations with admirable restraint and understanding. Mr. Sarin's contribution and involvement helps to lighten her load and cheer her up.

The Undesirable Homes

Just as we do not have any precise guidelines on which to build an 'ideal' home, similarly there are no established criteria to illustrate an undesirable home. But one can safely say that no child's personality can survive the trauma of a hostile family environment, or the catastrophe of a failed perent-child relationship.

Some families are unable to cope with the ordinary problems of daily existence. They may lack emotional, physical or financial strength to meet the demands of living. The inadequacies of these families may stem from the immaturity, lack of education, addictions (alcohol)or other such shortcomings of the parents. They keep floundering from one crisis to another as they lack 'self-direction', and thus are unable to control their own destinies.

Parental discord is a great cause of worry in children, who inevitably get embroiled in the conflict. Parents with grossly eccentric and abnormal personalities may keep the home in constant emotional turmoil. Due to their personal instability they are unable to give the child the required love and guidance. Parental irrationality and faulty behaviour is associated with a high incidence of psychological disorders among children. Such children also suffer from insecurity and low self-esteem.

It is not surprising that delinquency and other maladaptive behaviours are much more common in children and adolescents coming from incomplete (disrupted or broken) homes.

Children in frequently moving families are forced repeatedly to make adjustments with unfamiliar surroundings. Their schools, neighourhood and friends, with whom they build harmonious relationships, change and are lost. New adjustments can cause lot of anxiety and the child may become insecure and reticent.

Faulty parental attitudes (overindulgence, overprotection, strict discipline, unrealistic demands, and rejection) are responsible for a majority of personality disorders in children. Some of these maladaptive behavioural patterns, in the form of case studies, are discussed here.

Case Studies

Anirudh Singh, twelve, is an inconsiderate, whimsical little tyrant. He is self-centered, dominating, demanding and thoroughly spoilt. His parents treat him like a king and fulfill all his reasonable/unreasonable demands. His two elder sisters have clear instructions not to annoy him in any way.

Anirudh's father is 'living again' in his son, seeing him as a young replica of himself. He derives extreme satisfaction in gratifying any of his son's whims.

He is the apple of his mother's eye. She is not bothered that at twelve, her son already weighs over sixty kg.

Anirudh has learned to exploit his parents by skillfully crying, loving, being cute, well behaved or simply by throwing a tantrum, at which he is extremely crafty.

When Anirudh's important status at home was not reflected in the outside world, it came as a shock to him. Teased mercilessly by his peers and nick-named 'Fatso', he was confused initially but later developed very aggressive tendencies. He often fought with his schoolmates and rebelled against his teachers. His parents were reprimanded by the school-authorities but things did not improve. Gradually Anirudh become an anxious, unhappy, maladjusted child at school, while at home he remained a selfish, impatient brat.

Indulgent parents not only spoil their children but also spoil their chances of successful adjustments in life. Overpermissiveness and lack of discipline in the home has been correlated with antisocial, aggressive behaviour. In dealing with authority, such children are usually rebellious since for so long, they have had their own way.

Kunal Saxena, fourteen, is a fearful, dependent and submissive child. Right after birth his mother took control of his life and gave him little autonomy or freedom. Throughout infancy and childhood Kunal was kept in a

HOME: THE BASE CAMP

'germ free environment'. Children were uniformly not good enough to play with him—they were dirty, infectious, bad mannered or contaminating in some way or the other. Concept of 'hygiene' and fear of 'bacteria' are so deeply engrained in his mind that while going to school, picnic or movies, he might forget his spectacles but he never fails to carry his soap with him.

Kunal's mother doesn't want him to risk injury or face defeat by playing with 'evil' boys living in the neighbourhood. So he plays cricket with his father in their backyard. As it is Kunal is not allowed to remain outdoors much, because of his supposedly frail health. He is always overclothed, and medicines are poured down his throat with alarming regularity.

Till the age of four, Kunal was always carried in the arms of his parents. At six, he was still being breastfed at night. His mother would insist upon bathing him and putting on his clothes till he was twelve.

Maternal overprotection, or 'momism'—especially if the father is approving of, or complacent to, this 'smothering' of the child makes the child totally dependent. Such a child lacks initiative, seeks help whenever faced with any problem, avoids competition and does not derive satisfaction from work.

The four year old who does not feed himself, the five year old who doesn't play with peers unattended by the mother or the six year old who doesn't dress self are all exhibiting dependence.

In shielding the child from every danger, parents deny him the opportunities to learn by testing the realities.

Overprotection indirectly implies that they regard the child as incapable of coping with everyday problems. Such children grow up into insecure individuals, who feel threatened by the world. They have feelings of inadequacy, their intellectual striving is severely compromised and they generally suffer from low self-esteem.

Mayur Dwivedi, thirteen, has changed three schools in the last two years, due to poor performance in previous schools. He was admitted to the present one in the hope that, promised 'personalised attention' would help him overcome his problems. Here again he is lagging behind in the class without any signs of improvement.

During the last parent-teacher meeting Mr. Dwivedi showed his displeasure and disappointment at Mayur's grades. He complained that his hopes were belied, and the tall promises made at the time of admission and taking donation were not fulfilled.

Mrs. Prabha Mehra, the child counselor, attached to the school, was asked to talk to Mr. and Mrs. Dwivedi and take Mayur in her direct charge. The following report was submitted by Mrs. Mehra to the principal of the school:

Mr. Dwivedi, Deputy Superintendent Police, is a somewhat arrogant, irritable and easily excitable person who finishes all arguments with an emphatic wave of his hands. Mrs. Dwivedi is a timid, homely woman, who believes in walking one step behind her husband. Mr. Dwivedi returns home from his duty at odd unearthly hours. The slightest noise or disturbance at home makes him explode violently. He is a harsh disciplinarian who has a 'hands on' approach to all problems of children. He beats Mayur mercilessly on any pretext. During conversation Mr. Dwivedi declared with odd pride: "I don't have to hit Mayur anymore, my loud voice is enough to make him piss in his pants". Mayur is terrified of his father and suffers from anxiety, insecurity and feelings of worthlessness. He hates his father, and several times he has fantasised killing him with a knife. He has also contemplated running away from home. Mayur lacks initiative, spontaneity and is less friendly towards others. He lacks warmth in his dealing and tends to be aggressive. To get even with his father, he deliberately under performs in the examinations. He feels that this is one way by which he can get back at his father.

Six months and several counseling sessions later, Mr. Dwivedi was made to realise that his excessively harsh discipline and beatings were the reason behind Mayur's poor performance. It was his behaviour that required changing and not his child's schools. Thankfully Mr. Dwivedi changed his conduct and today Mayur is a happy child who is performing very well in his studies.

It has been well documented that punishment is associated with greater child dependency, more aggressiveness and a slower development of conscience. Extreme parental punitiveness makes the child emotionally unstable and less sociable. The unhappy effects of punishment run like a dismal thread throughout the later life of a child.

Gaurav Nigam is not even fifteen and already considers himself-a failure. Gaurav means 'glory'; this is what he was supposed to bring to the family. His parents are determined, upwardly mobile professionals who expect him to top in the class, excel in sports and win prizes in debates and dramatics. The Nigam household either has an air of 'great expectations' or of 'spectacular disappointments' linked to Gaurav's performance.

Initially, Gaurav tried to live up to his parents' unrealistically high expectations. But no matter how hard he tried he seemed to fail in the eyes of his parents. When he improved his rank from tenth to third, he was asked: "Why you didn't come first in the class?" Ultimately he couldn't cope with the sustained pressure and gave up. The unrealistic demands of his parents became his albatross. The painful frustration of not being good enough led to self-devaluation and Gaurav eventually came to feel: "I can't do it, so why try?"

By their excessive demands parents promote failure and also tend to discourage further effort on the part of the child. Where the child has the capacity for exceptionally high level performance, things may work out; but even here the child may be pushed so much that little room is left for spontaneity or development as an independent person. In some instances, parents who are not successful, focus on the child for meeting their own needs for success.

Esha Kumar, nine, is a shy, withdrawn and anxious child. She is the youngest of the three sisters and resents her more accomplished elder siblings. She is apprehensive of her mother, and unfortunately, her father has always been a stranger to the household.

By the time Esha arrived on the scene, Mrs. Kumar had already lost what ever little patience she had had with her two elder daughters. Esha thus faced rejection at a very early and vulnerable age. She was left at the mercy of a housemaid when she was hardly three months old. Throughout infancy and early childhood, Esha was looked after by a never-ending procession of maids. Even for her first day at school, her school bag and lunch box were arranged haphazardly by an illiterate maid.

At school Esha is well behaved to the point of being docile. Her grades are poor and she barely manages to scrape through. Her teachers find her dull, inactive and difficult to communicate with. Her standard response to most questions is, "I don't know". Esha doesn't have many friends, her only real friend is her doll; the two being inseparable. She goes to bed holding the doll in her arms and talks to her late into the night.

Mrs. Kumar, Esha's mother, is an aggressive, domineering woman with a harsh voice. She is given to expressing her opinion fervently and believes in having the last word in any argument. She is self-centered to the point of being selfish. She indulges herself with a lot of sleep, her kitty parties and card sessions. Shopping and going to movies with her friends are her favourite pastimes. With extreme dexterity she manipulates her entire home, her children and her businessman husband, to suit her life of leisure and irresponsible abundance.

Mrs. Kumar is fundamentally irritated by children and does not have much patience with her three daughters. For her the model child is the quiet, unobtrusive one-to be seen around the house, but not heard. She imposes strict discipline and rigid standards of behaviour. Her arbitrary commands always keep the children on tenterhooks and her sarcasm lashes out at them from every corner of the house.

Esha remains Mrs. Kumar's favourite victim. If she eats an ice cream her mother says, "I am sure you're going to spill it over your frock". If she opens the fridge for drinking water her mother says, "I suppose you are going to drop the bottle on the floor". If Esha sits down to do homework, Mrs. Kumar says, "I know you will make mistake in every line". Thus shattering little Esha's confidence with her harsh words and making her feel worthless.

Depending on her mood, Mrs. Kumar sometimes indulges in jokes and rough horseplay with the children, but when her good mood passes she flares up suddenly and comes down heavily on the girls. This irrational and unpredictable outburst confuses the children totally as to what is permitted and what is forbidden.

Esha's winning a prize in the painting competition at school was pooh-poohed by Mrs. Kumar. In her rush to attend a party she pushed away her daughter and her little trophy.

Most children subjected to maternal deprivation are not those separated from their mothers, but rather the ones who suffer from inadequate or distorted maternal care. Here the mother typically neglects the child, devotes little attention to him or her, and is generally rejecting of the child.

Rejection of the child may be done in various ways—by physical neglect, denial of love and affection, lack of interest in the child's activities and achievements, harsh or inconsistent discipline, failure to spend time with the child and lack of respect for the child's feelings. It may also involve cruel and abusive treatment of the child.

In Esha's case the rejections is:

- Complete (in majority of cases it is partial).
- Active (it is generally passive)
- Overtly cruel (subtly cruel form is more common).

Children of cold and rejecting mothers suffer from:

- Feeding problems
- Persistent bed-wetting
- Aggressiveness/excessive fears.
- Poor and slow conscience development.
- Diminished intelligence during early school years.
- Lying, stealing.
- Delinquency and running away from home.

And unpleasant emotional environment and lack of encouragement at home has a gross inhibiting and suppressing effect on a child's intellectual development and functioning. It is seen that many adults who were rejected in childhood have serious difficulty in giving and receiving affection.

In this sense, lack of love can be called a 'congenital disease'. Various studies show that parental rejection leads to feelings of insecurity and inadequacy, retarded conscience and general intellectual development, low self-esteem, loneliness and inability to give and receive love.

I have described 'home' as 'the base camp', a sanctuary,

from where the child should normally be able to operate safely and successfully. Can Esha's home be categorised as a 'Base Camp'? The most emphatic and obvious answer is NO! Let's get down to brass-tacks and analyse the situation in the Kumar household, in military fashion.

1. **Safety and Security**: A base camp should be well protected from enemy attacks. The Army does it by digging deep trenches, placing sandbags and by building concrete bunkers. The means used by a mother to strengthen her home are love, affection and emotional security. Sibling rivalries, and stress resulting from parent child maladjustment if not handled properly, have the potential to damage the base camp. Unfortunately for Esha, her base-of-operations, lacks the safety and security so essential to survive and succeed in this wily world.
2. **Ration:** Without sufficient rations no soldier can fight the enemy. Love, sympathy, understanding and stimulation all are strictly rationed in Esha's home. There is no way she can put up a decent fight on an affection-free diet.
3. **Ammunition:** To hold on to your base camp you need superior firepower. Esha lacks fire—in her thoughts as well as in her deeds. She neither has the will nor ambition to succeed, her self-esteem has been undermined by her own base commander. Poor Esha will have a tough time facing the world.
4. **Commander:** Base commander is the key figure as far as the well being of the camp and its inmates is con-

cerned. Mrs. Kumar should have facilitated emotional bonding and development of faith between the family members. On the contrary through her lack of interest and inconsistent and harsh discipline she has deliberately alienated them. Confusion, uncertainty, mistrust, doubts, dilemma and suspicion prevail in the Kumar household. Esha's base camp is vulnerable; it can fall to any adversary or adversity. Her defences are woefully inadequate, and her chances of success exceedingly slim.

According to George Santayana: "**The family is one of nature's masterpieces.**" Bright dreams of its members and dark realities of life compete with each other to colour this masterpiece. Family is a microcosm embracing intricate interpersonal relationships. The maintenance of dynamic equilibrium between the ambitions, demands and commands of the parents and the capabilities, strivings and performance of the children, is a must for sustenance of this little world.

5

School: The Battle Ground

Education is helping the child realise his potentialities
                                            Erich Fromm

Some prepares the child for future battles of life. Parental love and affection act as a 'protective shield', while proper guidance at school provides the 'ammunition'. A child's chances of success or failure in life depend largely upon these vital determinants. At the tender age of five, the young soldier is dispatched from his/her base camp to the battleground—popularly called 'School'. Thus begins the long and arduous journey through the varied experiences of formal schooling which brings the child into close interaction—concord/discord—with diverse personalities of a succession of teachers and of boys and girls from different backgrounds.

Most of the values and behaviour patterns are initiated at home; school environment merely establishes them — firmly and permanently. Favourable interactions at school make the child disciplined, hard working, helpful, well behaved and confident, while unfavourable school environment has the opposite effect. Unfortunate educational experiences, especially early on, can blaze a trail from which the child never diverges. Maladjustment in school guarantees that the child will develop a negative academic self-concept and increases the probabilities of child developing a generally poor self-image. Success or failure in school profoundly affects the child's personality. If the experiences of the first five or six years in school are positive, then this immunises the child against personality disorders for an indefinite period of time.

The nursery experience

Whenever I walk through the nearby forest nursery and look at little saplings, growing safely under the big shady trees, I am reminded of the nursery schools. The 'young saplings' if provided fertile soil and favourable environment, can grow into tall, strong, verdant trees. An unfavourable climate turns them into warped, dead wood.

Nursery school experience encourages the development of independence, initiative, intellectual curiosity and self-assertiveness. Children who attend nursery school are less inhibited, more spontaneous and more social. The social gains in nursery school provide sound foundations for further growth during the elementary-school years. Same is true for the 'early learning'; it forms the foundation upon which subsequent learning is based. A young child's mind is like an absorbent sponge, with tremendous capacity to absorb and retain. It must be allowed to mop-up as much information as possible.

How a nursery school affects the tender impressionable mind of a child depends largely upon the dynamic nature of teacher-child and child-child relationships. These interactions may either promote further growth, or they may impede and retard the child's social interests and skills.

What a nursery teacher school do:

- Establish a warm, friendly, personal relationship with the children.
- Arrange the play materials in ways that would help stimulate sustained co-operative play.
- Help the children in unobtrusive ways to make social and emotional adjustments amongst themselves.
- Give help and information more frequently.
- Ask more leading questions.
- Give simple constructive suggestions.

Formal education is not the primary aim of nursery schools, these schools are there to enhance the socialisation process of a child and to develop basic educational skills. Unfortunately nursery schools have become the 'training camps' for future battles to be fought in school battlegrounds. Children are being forced to write with pencils, unmindful of the calluses formed in small tender fingers. No one seems to mind the 'aborting' of 'free-flight' of the still raw but immensely imaginative brains by straitjacketing them.

School Life

School is a building that has four walls—with future inside.

Parents have inordinate faith in the advantages of sending their children to school They sincerely believe that in addition to formal education their child will learn right values and expected behaviour. They choose their child's school to the best to their ability and resources. They stand in endless queues and face innumerable interviews to get the best for their child. Would not it be an irony if the same school 'the temple of learning'— proved to be the nemesis of their child—'the temple of doom'?

Most of the children are enthusiastic about going to school, especially if an elder sibling is already studying there. It means a promotion for them and they evidence feelings of 'grown-upness' and self-importance. If the school environment is fascinating and they are able to have a harmonious relationship with their classmates and teachers, they integrate and adjust rapidly with their new life. It has been observed that the behaviour of such children improves. There is a tendency towards independence, helpfulness, responsibility and diligence.

A tryst with destiny—a child's first day at school

It's **Tina's** first day at school! The entire Verma household is reverberating with excitement, anxiety, apprehension and anticipation. Tina appears very tense and is crying incessantly since morning. On reaching the school she clings to her mother tightly and doesn't let go. Any attempt to reason, cajole or persuade her results in even bigger tears.

Tina is having acute 'separation anxiety' and is afraid that she may be separated from her parents permanently. Such scenes are a frequent phenomenon, repeated year after year on the first day of school. Separation anxiety, if not handled properly, can lead to school refusal and school phobia. Few simple measures and some prior preparation can make your child's first day at school a happy one.

1. Take your child to the school before the session starts and familiarise him/her with the surroundings.
2. Let the child see the swings and slides in the school playground. They are sure to interest and enthuse the child.
3. Tell the child about neighbourhood kids who go to the same school and help the child make friends with them.
4. If you plan to send your child by school bus, you should take him/her on the bus route a few times. Also show the bus stop from where he/she will board bus.
5. Leave the child occasionally with a friend or a relative for an hour or two. In this way he/she will get used to your absence and also learn that separation from you is only temporary.
6. Start a 'school going drill', a few days prior to the

opening of school. Make the child sleep and rise early, bathe in the morning and eat breakfast. Gradually the child will get used to this routine and will not face any difficulty when the school starts.
7. Motivate the child to go to school by describing your own pleasant experiences and memories of school.
8. Make it a point to receive your VIP after the school—at-least during the initial days.

Although school is primarily a place for learning, it also has an important role in the socialisation process of the child. A tubular vision equating schooling with mere education is not correct. Schools have the responsibility of transmitting the basic social values like a sense of co-operation, fair play, initiative, self-reliance, honesty and so on. Socialisation process necessarily involves the continued co-operation of parents. They shouldn't feel that they have discharged their primary responsibilities by simply sending the child to school. This is especially true of the parents who send their children to expensive, elitist boarding schools and leave the responsibility for the child's education and social adjustment to the school.

School life is a complex combination of many factors:

- Good, bad or indifferent teachers.
- Amicable, hostile or casual classmates.
- Pleasant, unpleasant or ambivalent school environment.
- Fascinating, dull or common place school activities.

- Realistic, unrealistic or confused parental expectations.
- Brilliant, poor or average achievement.

This list appears to be comprehensive, but is still incomplete. How these varied factors interact and influence the child's school life cannot be predicted. What is easier to predict is that no child can remain constantly indifferent or immune from his/her school influences.

It is true, the school provides a child with opportunities of learning, self expression and gratification of a variety of developmental needs, but it is also a source of some of the most disturbing conflicts. Peer associations and friendships forged during this period, last a lifetime and are unmatched in their capacity to provide emotional bonding, implicit faith and genuine understanding. Similarly the scars of traumatic experiences with unjust teachers, hostile classmates or repeated failures can never be entirely concealed or obliterated from memory; they keep haunting the psyche of the individual for rest of his/her life.

Maladjustment at school, whatever the reason, is an unfortunate but not an uncommon scenario. These children are caught in a mutual hate campaign with the school. Their rationalisation of 'poor teachers', 'dull books', 'boring classmates' are actually symptoms of their basic frustrations with schooling. Unfortunately, the teachers instead of helping them let them languish on the back-benches. Some excessively punitive teachers may target these children and victimise them unnecessarily, thus turning the hate campaign into an undeclared war.

The Underachiever

'Aptitude tests' are slowly but surely gaining currency in our country. I am convinced they are useful, especially if done by people with right intent and credentials. These tests are not a new thing; way back in seventies my school authorities had the vision to arrange them each year for the children entering Ninth standard. I remember, I was advised not to 'juggle' with numbers; I took biology instead and became a Pediatrician.

We also have standard tests of intelligence, which estimate the Intelligence Quotient or I.Q. of an individual. The term 'underachiever' is used to indicate the child whose academic performance falls below the level of his/her assessed I.Q. Why should this happen? Obviously, the child is being forced to do something for which he/she hasn't got the aptitude.

This is not the only cause for underachievement. Children from lower socio-economic strata and large families are generally underachievers. It also holds good if the parents are not well educated, especially if the mother is a school dropout owing to a lack of encouragement and stimulation for academic excellence.

Achievement in school is closely related to the 'level of aspiration', i.e. how well a child wishes to perform in the future, compared to how well he had done in the past. Level of aspiration is closely related to self-image and is directly proportional to the motivation and confidence level of the child. Success acts as a catalyst in this process; it increases the level of aspiration by increasing confidence and optimism. Persistent failure results in resignation, pessimism and lowering the of level of aspiration.

With the development of conscience, children gradually become achievement oriented. Their motivation comes from within, and they start experiencing an urge to excel and make their parents proud and teachers happy. For this condition to develop, it is necessary for children to look up-to their parents and teachers as socially, intellectually and economically superior; as people who are dependable; as those who love them and who value their success. Unless a child has this inner drive to perform well, no amount of cajoling, compelling, enticement or punishment will work. A child, who does not value success in school, generally becomes an underachiever.

Success in school is also affected by and is closely related to the aspiration levels of parents. The aim of the parents should be that their children do better than them in life. This becomes the aim of the children and they start striving harder. Competition with parents may not be strong in children from lower socio-economic strata, since their parents are at the bottom of the social hierarchy.

Specialised test arrangements with easy beginning, informal and relaxed settings and memory supports are suggested as means to help the underachievers. Parents must provide motivation and emotional support to these children and should work in close co-operation with the school.

The Dream School

Schools with comfortable buildings, plenty of educational and recreational facilities, uniformly delight all children. In addition to providing children with opportunities for all round development, they also give them a feeling of belonging and pride. In contrast schools with nondescript, dilapidated buildings, small, dark and unventilated classrooms are sure to discourage and depress children. The effect of such schools on the mental and intellectual growth of children is bound to be adverse if not calamitous.

Schools should promote group activities like morning prayers, song/dance, physical training and team games. These not only provide children with opportunities to display their talents but also teach them the advantages of working together, co-operation and sharing.

The school should aim at providing maximum opportunities for the maximum number of children. A good school 'organises success' for everyone, especially the less able, while facilitating the illumination of its luminaries— the bright students. Children who win prizes in various competitions must be given due recognition by organising prize distribution functions.

Scout groups, National Cadet Corps, trekking and hiking trips must be organised in the school. These group activities allow close interaction among children and stimulate learning process. It brings them in close contact with nature and helps in the development of robust physiques and sharp reflexes.

The most important and vital asset of any school is not its grand building, but a set of dedicated teachers, who understand the principles of psychological and cognitive development in children and apply them earnestly. A dream school must ensure that its teachers have a clear understanding of children's behaviour; without this knowledge effective teaching is not possible.

Teacher-Pupil Interaction

If the classroom is a stage, the teacher is the master of ceremonies. If the classroom becomes a circus, teacher has to be the ringmaster. All in all, teacher remains the undisputed conductor of class-room orchestra. Mind you! the wailing, shouting and synchronised cacophony of some classrooms can put many a rock band to shame.

As mentioned before, initially, almost all children look favourably upon going to school. A vast majority of children in later school years still remain positive about and fascinated by their school, but a significant number of them develops ambivalent views. Although they still say that they like the school, they do not consider going to school a pleasant activity. They like school because they believe that education would help them in later life. Why do so many children develop an antipathy towards school life? The majority of children who actively dislike school attribute their negative feelings to the behaviour of their teachers.

The teachers have important influences on children's intellectual competencies, academic achievements, social values and behaviour patterns. Many successful adults attribute their accomplishments to childhood contacts with helpful, understanding and sympathetic teachers. On the contrary, many unsuccessful adults blame their failures and social maladjustment on the spitefulness and unkind behaviour of their teachers and hold them responsible for their truancy and stultified school life. There is little doubt that teachers do have a potent effect on the growth of majority of children. Since this is the case, it is important to know what kind of teachers are liked and disliked by pupils.

Idealised Teacher–The Creator:

According to A.T. Jersild, children like those teachers best who have the following characteristics:

- Human qualities—kind, cheerful, good tempered and natural.
- Disciplinarian qualities—fair, consistent, impartial and respected.
- Physical appearance—well groomed, nice voice and generally attractive.
- Teaching qualities—helpful, democratic (give children a say in class affairs), interesting and enthusiastic.

A quick scan of the above list tells us that teachers who help children to satisfy their social and intellectual needs, will be liked and admired. Most children want their teachers to be nice, kind, friendly, understanding, willing to help and fair. The ability to explain things lucidly is a major asset of a teacher. Teachers, who are approachable, open to ideas and generally have time for the pupil's problems are not only loved but worshipped.

One essential quality missing in many teachers is the ability to see the funny side of innumerable eminently laughable situations in the classroom. Teachers who let children laugh when something is funny, and believe in having fun with them are the preferred ones.

Teachers are vital instillers of confidence and self-worth in their charges. Parents initially, and teachers subsequently, have to help the child to savour the first tiny taste of triumph to encourage further effort. These little victories add up into major success later on in life. Such children develop positive self-image and are not afraid of failures. By attempting and succeeding at tough tasks they develop into confident achievers.

Disliked Teacher: The Saboteur

Teachers who uniformly thwart their pupils' needs or who set goals which are unattainable by the majority of the children are generally disliked. Probably the most avidly disliked teachers are the ones who not only set goals which the children cannot attain, but also force the children to achieve them by threats and punishment.

A disliked teacher shows the following traits:
- Scolds pupils a lot.
- Is usually cross and bossy.
- Always tries to find faults.
- Has no words of encouragement.
- Is easily irritated.
- Is prejudiced and unfair.
- Doesn't give freedom of expression and scope for improvisation.

SCHOOL: THE BATTLE GROUND

- Is punitive beyond reason and without being helpful.
- Gives too much homework.

Attitudes, prejudices, conflicts and personal social values of teachers are unavoidably translated into behaviour patterns of children. Although the teacher is the primary source of approval and disapproval, there exists a dynamic teacher-pupil interaction within the confines of the classroom. The teacher may label the pupils as— bright, dumb, compliant, wild, eager and disinterested. Similarly pupils also label their teachers as kind, vicious, attractive, unattractive, interesting, boring, reasonable and unreasonable.

An important role of the teacher, especially in the primary classes, is to promote the development of a positive self-concept in children. This is possible only if he or she distributes approval and disapproval in a consistent and equitable manner. Unfortunately, a select group of children receive most of the teacher's approval. This discrimination —intentional or otherwise—opens the door for success for a select few, but shuts it tightly in the face of others.

Proper orientation of such teachers is urgently called for, because not only are they doing nothing to improve an already intolerable situation for frustrated and maladjusted children, but are actively damaging their future.

Why do some teachers behave in this manner? The causes are many and reasons varied.

The favoured child may be

- Taking private tuition from the teacher.
- From a very well connected family.
- A ward of some faculty member.

Some teachers are themselves socially maladjusted and punitive by nature. They release their pent-up anger and aggressive tendencies by abusing the most defenseless children in their classrooms. Also, because of their own inadequacies and lack of confidence they become unnecessarily and excessively annoyed by children who seem to threaten their role as disciplinarians and leaders in the classroom. Children suffer intense frustration and pain as these teachers vent their aggressive tendencies through sarcasm, threat and physical punishment.

Case Study:

Aditi, a grade V student, was brought to me by her parents with complaints of intractable tremors in her right hand. The tremors started suddenly, there was no other complaint and the child was generally healthy. I examined her carefully but could not find anything wrong. A prescription for a mild sedative and multivitamins did the trick.

After three months the child was back again with even more violent tremors. This time the 'tranquilisers' failed to fully control her tremors, which appeared and disappeared erratically. Various investigations including a CT Scan showed no abnormality. A detailed history revealed that Aditi's tremors had a direct association with her examinations; they always preceded them. On gentle probing, she came out with a terrible tale of severe caning on her hands, by her teacher for performing badly in the examinations. Counseling of the child along with a change of 'section' made her tremors disappear permanently.

Most teachers are not unfair, prejudiced or malevolent, they simply get exasperated and frustrated by non-confirming, withdrawn and apathetic children. The patience of a teacher is put to litmus test while dealing with children who are slow learners. The problem is more compounded in the present day classrooms where sixty or more children clamour for the attention of a single teacher.

The Classmates: Comrades up in arms

Parents lay the foundations for social behaviour; teachers modulate it, but it is the peer group, which enables the child to develop and practice the skills of co-operation and competition, independence and dependence, and leadership and team spirit. Interactions with and acceptance by peers constitute a very important stage in the development of the child. Peers may form an important part of the success equation or they may precipitate failure.

The financial status of the peer group plays an important role in shaping the feelings of well being or otherwise. Children who are not able to match their peers as per trendy clothes, bikes or other material possessions like a stylish school bag or water bottle can get an inferiority complex regarding their presumed poverty. Parents must swiftly counter these damaging tendencies by explaining the disadvantages of getting into unnecessary and wasteful competition. However, no child should be denied reasonable requests and perhaps some unreasonable ones too.

Sometimes children of affluent parents, especially the ones with no worthwhile achievement to their name, try to impress their peers by splurging money. They attract the vulnerable children by treating them in fast food joints, taking them to movies and allowing them to use their jazzy bikes. Later they exploit these children by involving them in nefarious activities. They teach them to drink, smoke, lie and steal, thus slowly but surely pushing them on the path of delinquency.

Bullying and teasing in school can have a catastrophic effect on academic performance and on life in general. If this menace is not dealt with firmly and in time, it can play havoc with the confidence and self-image of the child. Something as trivial as a dark complexion, odd surname, longish nose or thick spectacles can lead to teasing. Bullying—which may sadly originate from teaching staff— can cause an inferiority complex with may not be easily overcome even in later life.

Untidiness and unfashionable clothes serve to invite the unwelcome attention of classmates. Personality traits like frequent blinking of eyes, stuttering or stammering are a frequent cause of harassment. These children are already vulnerable from a psychological point of view; relentless teasing and bullying can cause severe damage to their psyche.

The significance of unkindness and cruelty should

never be underestimated and the child's perception of it never dismissed. Teachers and parents must act in tandem to protect the child from this scourge. They should keep an eye on the child's behaviour and should remain especially vigilant for signs of anxiety and apprehension. Peer group activities of the child must be monitored discreetly, and all possible communication channels utilised to help the child. If properly planned intervention is delayed the child's personality development may be seriously undermined. Timidity and delinquency are natural corollaries of the personality derangement.

Case Study:

Aasif, a class Tenth student, was average in studies but very good in sports. He was the eldest of four children in the household, which also included his aged grandparents. His father was a clerk in a government office, who somehow managed to make the two ends meet.

During annual sports meet Aasif won the best athlete's award. He was befriended by some well-to-do senior boys of the school and they soon became a close group which could be seen huddled together in all corners of the school. Aasif started smoking and bunking classes for trips to movies and restaurants with his group. He and his friends were frequent visitors to the expensive discotheques of the city. Aasif was amazed and dazed by the endless supply of cash his friends had.

This continued throughout the year, at the end of which Aasif was debarred from appearing in the board examinations, because his attendance fell short of the required minimum. Out of anxiety and apprehension he kept this hidden from his father. During the examination days he would go out of the house on the pretext of giving papers and return with the examination paper of a friend. On the day of the result he committed suicide.

It is extremely difficulty to identify, quantify and evaluate exactly what went wrong and where? What hereditary-environmental variables combine to distort and blight a child's personal-social growth? What makes some boys to play truant at school or become juvenile delinquents, while others become model students and responsible citizens?

To 'search' for the cause, we will have to first open the 'home page'. Faulty home environment may be the reason for the child's maladjustment at school. Further searches must be made at the school site, where the child may be rejected and harassed by teachers and classmates. Afraid, bored, confused, prejudiced, abused and inappropriately taught, the child falls short of expected standards and is promptly labelled as a failure.

Our educational system brutally rejects those who fall short of the supposed norms. Rejection and failure in school may generate within the child vicious hatred and revolt against a system that seems to exist to frustrate him. It is too clear today that the number of these thwarted, rejected and angry young people is on the increase, to the great detriment of society and themselves.

Optimum harmony between the school and home results in maximum benefits to the child. Close involvement of the parents in the schooling of their child is of utmost importance if the child has to rise above the ordinary. Parent-teacher meetings are significant opportunities through which teachers can interact simultaneously with the parents and child. These occasions must be utilised not only to discuss the present performance of the child but also to plan for the future. If a child's weaknesses and problem areas are being highlighted, remedial measures should also be suggested. Teachers must never forget to inform the parents about the interests and strengths of the child.

Although maladjustment and failures in school are lamentable, they should not blind us to the commendable success with which schools generally are able to determine the social growth and academic achievements of majority of children. The desired role of education should not be to spotlight individual weaknesses but to provide opportunity and stimulation for every child. Anatole France had said: *"The whole art of teaching is the art of awakening the natural curiosity of young minds for the purpose of satisfying it afterwards."* Let this be the engraved motto of each school, the solemn oath of each teacher and the sole objective of our educational system.

6

The Problem Child

When discipline turns into punishment, problems of the child increase.

P.K.

A child, who is difficult to deal with, at home and school, is promptly labelled a 'problem child' and branded lazy, stubborn, irresponsible, impulsive, untidy, careless, poor learner, inattentive etc. Tragically the post-script to the above accusations may include derogatory words like fool, idiot and moron.

The problem child in fact, is a child 'with problems', some of which are quite incapacitating. Attention Deficit/Hyperactivity Disorder (Short Attention Span), Learning Disability, Partial Sensory Loss (hearing, visual) and Severe Emotional Stress—all can affect the child's performance.

Children are always under parental and social pressure to perform. The standards and norms of academic achievement and social behaviour respectively, are set by a rigid adult society, which is quite unrelenting in its attitudes and values. It, generally, is unable to view things from a child's perspective, preference and potential. It remains a mystery how adults develop amnesia to their childhood inadequacies. If a child fails to confirm to the 'social prescription', he/she is condemned post-haste.

Instead of blaming the child, parents and teachers should be willing to admit that a problem exists; acknowledging a problem is the first step towards solving it. The real reason for poor academic performance or inappropriate conduct must be identified as soon as possible, because the longer the problem persists, greater the damage. Professional help of a child psychologist may be required to define the problem and its extent. Early identification and timely intervention can help children to overcome the deficit and thrive inspite of their disability.

Learning Disabled Child

Is your child like **Tanvi**?
1. **Tanvi** knows the schedule of most TV serials, the lyrics of all popular songs, the winners and runners up of various national and international beauty pageants but forgets the table of five, simple rules of grammar and her home assignment day after day. This selective amnesia is used by her to avoid frustrating academic work.
2. The prospect of tackling her maths homework makes Tanvi shudder with apprehension. She becomes so

tense that she just can't seem to get started. She takes out her books, puts back the wrong ones and spends a lot of time selecting proper pens and pencils. Suddenly she becomes very thirsty and goes for a drink, and then she goes to the bathroom, but never really starts her assignment.

3. Tanvi generally takes hours to complete her homework, with frequent breaks for resting her tired fingers and burning eyes. She sharpens her pencil constantly in the elusive pursuit of a fine tip and a finer handwriting. She readily agrees to go to the kitchen for finishing her milk but takes an eternity to come back. Mother's presence by her side makes her plod through the work, but at the slightest opportunity she slinks away.

4. Occasionally Tanvi finishes her homework very quickly, with little if any care or patience. It may be the time for her favourite TV show or simply to free herself from the tension of pending assignment. She is not bothered whether her work is inaccurate or incomplete.

5. Tanvi frequently brings home unfinished class-work: many answers are incomplete, several sums are unsolved. She generally manages to hide the adverse remarks but if caught, blames the teacher for speaking very fast or the pen for writing slowly. She constantly leaves long-term assignments and holiday homework until the last minute.

6. Teachers complain that Tanvi is inattentive, talkative, leaves her seat frequently and annoys other children.

It seems she deliberately gets into trouble, in the hope of getting out of the classroom.
7. The commonest remark made by teachers in Tanvi's report card is 'could do better'. This in fact, has been part and parcel of her school experience right from the beginning.
8. Tanvi has visited several Pediatricians, Ophthalmologists and Gastroenterologists for her frequent headaches and stomachaches. She generally complains of feeling ill before going to school especially during the examinations.

Children like Tanvi are obviously experiencing problems with learning. The inability to cope with the demands of school curriculum leads to development of 'avoidance behaviour'. These children try their level best to avoid academic work because of the possibility of perceived failure, loss of parental approval and peer humiliation.

As determined by various IQ tests the average intelligence of general population falls within the range of 90-110. Children with learning disability usually have an IQ within or above this range. A child with learning disability may have deficits in one or more of the following areas:

- Reading comprehension
- Listening comprehension
- Written expression
- Oral expression
- Mathematical computation

- Mathematical reasoning

According to a rough estimate about 5% of the school going children may suffer from learning disability. It must be made amply clear that these children do not have a low I.Q., emotional problems, visual or hearing deficits. Several theories have been propounded regarding the cause of learning disabilities. Some of the better-accepted ones center around, heredity, complications of pregnancy and subtle neurological impairments. It seems these children have faulty brain wiring, causing cross connections and confusion. While it is not mandatory, many children with learning disability may have other relatives or family members who exhibit the same type of problems.

Important tips for parents

1. A child can't suddenly develop learning disability in fifth grade. With true learning disability a previous history of educational problems right from the time of nursery school is generally present. These children may also have history of delayed early development e.g. Language delays.
2. A child can be learning disabled in one or more areas i.e. mathematical computation, spelling or written expression. It goes without saying: the more areas affected, more serious the disability.
3. Difficulty in distinguishing left from right, b from d, was from saw, 6 from 9 is commonly seen in children upto the age of five years and may not indicate any

learning disability. However, if a child frequently reverses letters and numbers even after the age of seven, professional help should be sought.

4. Dyslexia and learning disability are not the same and should not be confused with each other. Dyslexics have a specific severe problem in learning how to read (Dys=difficulty with, lexis=words). All dyslexic children are learning disabled but all learning disabled children are not dyslexic.

Helping a learning disabled child

1. Learning disabled children have certain areas of severe weakness but they also have certain areas of strength. Some children learn better by seeing (Visual Learners), some by listening (Auditory Learners), some by feeling (Tactile Learners), and some by a combination of these methods. This can be found out by providing them with several alternative methods of learning e.g. Audio tape, Video tape, Slides, Flips Charts, Bulletin Board, Demonstrations, Field trips, Debates, Discussions, Projects, Role playing etc.
2. If shorter assignments are given the child will have better chance of success. Success is absolutely necessary for these children, otherwise due to fear of failure they may avoid academic work.
3. Assignments can be presented in the form of small units of three problems or a paragraph or two of written work at a time. Give immediate feedback if the child is doing the assignment incorrectly. This saves time and energy and prevents frustration.

4. Parents can provide a highlighter pen to the child to underline important facts and circle the difficult words. This type of input enhances child's memorising ability.
5. These children should preferably be allowed to sit in the front rows of the class. This allows the teacher to provide frequent inputs to the child and reinforce them from time to time. Another advantage is that by sitting close to the teacher, the child is separated from the distracting influence of other children.
6. The teacher can put the child with a peer helper to help with class work. Although a bit difficult to implement, it is a very practical and useful option for the teachers.
7. Providing the child with a time-table to finish work helps in many cases. Dividing the assignment into specific time slots provides the child with a structured environment to work in. Accomplishing the task step by step allows the child to remain focused and motivated. Use of a 'Daily Study Roster' is very helpful for children with learning disability and is highly recommended.

Hyperactive Child

Rahul, eight, is an inattentive, impulsive and a hyperactive child who is facing serious academic, social and disciplinary problems. He often fails to finish things he starts, doesn't seem to listen and is easily distracted. Because of poor concentration he makes frequent careless mistakes. He frequently loses books, copies, pens and pencils. He has difficulty in staying seated, is fidgety and keeps shifting from one activity to another. He is always running about or climbing things and needs a lot of supervision.

Daily Study Roster
Name: Tanvi   **Study Target: 2 Hours Daily**

Day	Date	Subject	Time Slots 30 Mts	30 Mts	30 Mts	30 Mts	Remarks
Monday	2.7.2001	Maths Social-Studies	✗	✗	✗	✓	Unsatisfactory
Tuesday	3.7.2001	Science, English	✗	✓	✓	✓	Satisfactory
Wednesday	4.7.2001	Maths, English	✗	✗	✓	✓	Unsatisfactory
Thursday	5.7.2001	Social-Studies, Science	✗	✓	✗	✓	Unsatisfactory
Friday							
Saturday							

- ✓ Denotes compliance ✗ denotes avoidance/non compliance.
- The child studies for only 30 minutes at a stretch.
- After every half-hour check the child's work, ask questions from the allotted chapter.
- Child should be allowed flexibility in choosing time slots and subjects.
- After the completion of all four time slots give remarks: Good/Satisfactory/Unsatisfactory

Rahul is suffering from attention deficit/hyperactivity disorder (ADHD), which accounts for the largest category of psychological referrals among children. This disorder affects about 5% of the primary school children, with 75% or more being boys. The exact cause of ADHD is not known but it seems to be a genetic disorder. There is presumptive evidence of minimal brain damage, which in most cases is genetically inherited, but could also be due to complications during pregnancy and birth. A history of learning or conduct problems is commonly found in a parent or close relative of children with ADHD. Early identification and prompt intervention is crucial for these children, as it can prevent maladjustment at home and with the peer group.

Managing a Hyperactive Child

A. General Principles

Although general principles of management are useful, individualised care for each child achieves greater success. Effective treatment depends upon close co-operation and constant communication between the psychotherapist, parents and school. This helps to reduce frustration and feelings of helplessness in the child, as well as care providers.

1. When a hyperactive child acts or behaves impulsively in a socially incorrect manner, don't just point out the mistake but try to explain the inappropriateness of behaviour to the child. Reinforce proper behaviour immediately by praise or gift because waiting too long

to reward the child may blunt the desired effect.
2. Initially, hyperactive children should be exposed to small group interactions. Because of better control and less distraction they are able to accomplish simple tasks and feel successful. This gives them the confidence to progress to more difficult academic work.
3. Parents and teachers should try to identify strengths of the child that can be publicly announced or praised. This not only boosts the child's morale but also changes the negative mindset of other children.
4. A hyperactive child finds it difficult to remain seated for an extended period of time. The teacher can arrange to have the child run an errand: cleaning the black board, distributing checked copies etc. This allows the child to leave the seat for a purposeful activity and generates feelings of importance and accomplishment.
5. At home, an alarm clock can be used to deal with the problem of seating the child for an extended period. Make a deal with the child that he will get up only after the alarm goes off. Initially set the alarm for 30 minutes and subsequently increase it to 45 minutes or one hour. The anticipation of being allowed to leave the seat motivates the child to remain seated. This conditioning exercise succeeds with most children and should also help your child.
6. Hyperactive children are generally disorganised and frequently forget to copy the homework. They also have problems in listening and taking notes. Parents must establish close co-operation with teachers and

request them to spare a few minutes to verify whether the child has completed class-work and taken down the home assignment or not. Occasionally, the teacher may provide the child with extra time for completing work. Help of a friend may also be taken and the incomplete work can be xeroxed from his/her copy.
7. These children keep their things in a very disorderly manner. They should be helped in arranging the books and notebooks, organising the study table and cleaning the drawers. Encourage the child to make it a weekly task.
8. Designate the study area. Do not allow the child to study in all corners of the house in a haphazard manner. To prevent distraction and improve concentration, put off the room lights and use a table lamp. Treating the study area as sacred (by removing slippers, lighting incense) may help in motivating the child.
9. Avoid giving multiple instructions and assignments simultaneously. Allow the child to carry out one direction or finish one assignment, before going on to the next one. Some children get flustered by seeing too many problems on the same page. Take a sheet of paper and cover the rest while allowing the child to tackle one problem at a time.
10. Permitting the child to use graph paper while doing arithmetic work provides a structured format in which to place numbers. Large graph paper should be used so that the child can easily place one number in each box. This helps the child to approach the task in a

systematic manner. There is no harm in allowing these children to use calculators. They can also be provided with basic math tables and formulas while doing their assignment. The aim here is to successfully accomplish the task at hand, by avoiding frustration of not being able to remember and recall the facts.

11. Some children grasp better if provided with auditory and visual inputs simultaneously. Parents can tape-record a chapter so that the child can read and listen at the same time.

12. Computers are rapidly gaining access in our homes, and the child should be familiarised with them at the earliest. Computers can be used to organise the child's work, to teach typing skills and to improve word power by using various packages readily available in the market. This machine is fascinating, addicting as well as motivating. The child will feel very good about himself, especially on seeing a report generated by his/her own effort.

13. Organise your child's things at night to avoid stress and confusion before going to school in the morning. Ask the child to develop a checklist, so that the school dress, books, copies and home assignment are ready for the next morning. This will help the child to feel secure as he/she reaches the school better prepared.

14. Parents must be realistic about their expectations from the child and should ignore minor incidents and focus on the major areas of concern. They should familiarise themselves with situations which are frustrating to the child. Avoiding confrontation and

providing emotional support is the right approach during these moments.

B. Psychotherapy

Psychotherapy helps the child to:
- gain in self-esteem
- release pent up frustration
- control impulsiveness

Psychotherapists use 'behaviour modification' to control hyperactivity and improve the concentration of the child. This mode of treatment involves a system of incentives and deterrents, daily report cards etc. Some people also recommend family therapy.

C. Special Diet

Dr. Ben Feingold put forward a hypothesis linking hyperactivity to the use of artificial colours and flavours, preservatives and naturally occurring substances in food called salicylates. He postulated that eliminating these substances from the child's diet would result in remission of the problem. However, subsequent research has failed to substantiate Dr. Feingold's dietary theory. Treatment of A.D.H.D. by special diets has raised a great deal of controversy and further research in this area is required.

D. Medication

Most commonly used psycho-stimulants for ADHD are Dexedrine and Ritalin. Unfortunately they are not available in India, though Dexedrine was available some twenty years back, but has since been withdrawn from the market. These drugs improve concentration and increase the child's awareness of the world around him/her. More than half the children exhibit a decrease in unwanted symptoms and almost ten per cent show a dramatic improvement in their behaviour. It should be kept in mind that these drugs do not cure the disorder but alleviate troublesome symptoms. Common side effects seen in the use of these drugs are nausea, loss of appetite and weight loss. There is some concern that use of psycho-stimulant drugs may lead to drug dependency/abuse, although there is no research to prove this.

Emotionally Disabled Child

Jenny, a grade V student, was very punctual and did quite well in her first terminal examination. Gradually she started being late and was frequently absent from school. Quite often she would refuse to separate from her parents at the school gate. She started doing incomplete work, which was full of careless mistakes. She performed badly in subsequent examinations and failed in two subjects. She became withdrawn from peers and started blaming them along with the teachers for her poor performance.

Jenny constantly visited the school dispensary with complaints of headache or pain in abdomen. In the classroom her common refrain to any problem was, "I don't know" or "I can't do it." This downward trend in her performance continued unabated and culminated in her failing the final examination.

Jenny had suffered a severe emotional trauma because of the death of her younger brother after prolonged hospitalisation. She had developed an obsessive fear of death and was perpetually imagining herself to be suffering from some fatal illness. Her grief stricken parents failed to recognise Jenny's emotional turmoil. This resulted in another setback to the family in the form of Jenny's academic failure.

Jenny represents a child experiencing severe emotional stress, resulting in social, environmental and academic maladjustment. Her dynamic state of tension adversely affected her learning abilities and resulted in failure. Several other situations can cause emotional stress in a child; some of the important ones are listed below.

Important causes of emotional stress in a child:

- Peer pressure and peer rejection
- Parental discord or divorce
- Parental loss of job
- Change in environment due to shifting of family
- Death in the family
- Health related problems
- Abuse
- High parental expectations
- Sibling performance
- Cultural and language difficulty
- Inability to follow teacher's instructions
- Repeated school failure

Common symptoms seen in an emotionally disabled child:

- Academic underachievement inspite of good potential
- Frequent absence from school
- Poor social skills leading to peer rejection
- Constant complaints of headaches, stomachache etc.
- Low confidence and poor self worth
- Excessive fears and phobias
- Impulsive, aggressive or confrontational behaviour

Dealing with an Emotionally Disabled Child

Emotional disorders may vary from mild to severe, but they usually interfere with academic performance. Try to understand the child's problems and search for solutions. You can solve many perplexing behavioural riddles at your own level by your sincere efforts. It is crucial to tackle emotional stress at the earliest; allowing it to linger on can permanently damage the child's personality.

1. The basic principle of reinforcing positive behaviour by rewarding it, while fixing some penalty or unpleasant consequence for inappropriate behaviour, remains the most effective tool for dealing with these children. Work out a contract with your child regarding accepted behaviour and rewards. Consequences for breaking the rules, previously agreed upon, should also be fixed.
2. Try using a chart with a point system to visually project the child's pattern of punctuality/lateness and complete/incomplete academic work. This increases the child's awareness and sense of responsibility, while

decreasing denial and avoidance behaviour. The chart can be used universally for all children to improve behaviour and performance.

Weekly Performance Chart

Name: Jenny   **Grading: Poor**

Day	Date	Punctual/Late or Absent	Assignment complete/ incomplete	Point
Monday	2.7.2001	0	0	0
Tuesday	3.7.2001	5	5	10
Wednesday	4.7.2001	5	0	5
Thursday	5.7.2001	0	0	0
Friday	6.7.2001	0	0	0
Saturday	7.7.2001	5	5	10
		Total Points		**25**

Scoring System:

Punctuality at school   = 5
Late or absent from school   = 0   Maximum achievable
                                      score = 60
Assignment complete   = 5
Assignment incomplete   = 0

Grading and Reward/Intervention:

Points	Grade	Reward/Intervention
60	Excel-Lent	Extra Time to Play and Watch TV, Favourite Book Comic or Chocolates, Sunday Outing with Ice Cream
55	Good	Extra Time to Play and Watch TV, Favourite Books and Comic, Sunday Outing. No Chocolates or Ice Cream
50	Fair	Extra Time to Play
45	Average	Provide Motivation to Improve Performance
40 or Less	Poor	Extra time for Studies, Motivation, Emotional Support

3. Emotionally disabled children have a feeling of hopelessness and become easily frustrated. If their homework is unfinished or they can't find a book they will resist going to school. Parent should check homework and other assignments during the night and ensure that the child is adequately prepared for school. Leaving very little for morning makes the child relax and go to school with confidence.
4. If an emotionally disturbed child is provided with sufficient opportunities to verbalise his/her concerns and seek help, a tendency towards inappropriate behaviour is reduced dramatically. The child should be approached as often as possible and gently persuaded to speak about his/her problems and fears. It is not a bad idea to fix a specific time when the child can talk to the parent alone. This reduces frustration and allows the child to unwind and think positively.

5. The teacher should always praise punctuality, good behaviour and up-to-date class work. A positive comment, verbal or written, can do wonders for the child's confidence and application.
   The class teacher should try to detach the child from those children who bother or provoke him/her. This pre-emptive measure reduces the child's anxiety and the consequent feeling of security facilitates learning.
6. Emotionally disabled children shirk social interaction. They avoid outdoor activities, where they may have to deal with other children. Initially, expose your child to a small group of one or two children. As the child grows in confidence and becomes comfortable, increase the group size. You can choose some constructive activity or a simple project for the group and occasionally place the child in a leadership role.

Finally

It is not uncommon to come across impulsive, disorganised, forgetful, inattentive children who appear to merely 'float around in time'. They are not likely to accomplish much without their parents giving them direction, facilitating their learning, enriching their experiences and defining their goals. Good parenting is all about this, and more!

7

The Abused Child

What a child doesn't receive he can seldom later give.

PD James

Child abuse has been a societal phenomenon for centuries but its true magnitude is only now being understood. It is found in all societies and is almost always a highly guarded secret wherever it takes place. Child abuse has been the subject of extensive studies by social scientists, psychologists and pediatricians in recent years. We will look at some important aspect of child abuse and how it prevents a child from realising his/her potential.

Severe physical abuse, especially fatal cases, do come to light, but many milder cases go undetected or unreported so that it is hard to obtain accurate data on their incidence. Sexual abuse is often hidden within families; it may not be revealed until the victim speaks of it in later life. This may happen during psychotherapy for some psychiatric problem. Emotional abuse is extremely difficult to detect, define and prove.

It is a misconception that child abuse is restricted to lower socio-economic strata of the society only. Children from seemingly 'perfect' middle and upper class homes are by no means exempt from this malady. They also face physical violence, emotional trauma and sexual exploitation. The difference is more of degree and frequency than an absolute one. Even the so-called prestigious schools of the affluent are a breeding ground for physical, sexual and emotional abuse of children.

Abuse can start right after conception! If a mother lacks emotional support, proper nourishment and rest during pregnancy and receives substandard care at the time of delivery her baby's wellbeing is likely to be compromised. The baby may have low birth weight, suffer birth injuries or there may be a delay in establishing respiration. These babies run the risk of developing sub-clinical brain damages, which can result in learning disabilities, short attention span and academic failures.

The perpetrators of violence or sexual abuse are often 'trusted' individuals, usually male family members in a position of authority. Children, who are victims, can themselves become abusers in later life. They may be physically violent to children in their care or to their own children.

Causation

1. Lack of parenting skills, particularly in the ability to respond to the young child's developmental needs combined with unrealistic expectations regarding the stage of a child's development often results in physical violence. The cause for abuse may be a minor one—persistent crying, feeding difficulties or toilet training accidents. Parents may feel that the child is deliberately provoking and thwarting them.
2. Cultural acceptance of corporal punishment and inherent violence within the society greatly affects the incidence of child abuse. In some societies there is an excessive reliance on harsh discipline and physical punishment while dealing with children.
3. An unwanted child especially with the background of financial pressures and unemployment is at high risk of abuse.
4. Unsupported and socially isolated, single parent homes can ring with the cries of abused children.
5. Child abuse is a natural corollary of 'substance abuse' on the part of parents. There is a strong association between domestic violence, sexual abuse and an alcoholic father.
6. Child abuse is almost a certainty when parents themselves have been abused and neglected as children. Their unconscious model of parenthood is a violent one and they instinctively see physical punishment as the preferred way of dealing with undesired behaviour in children.

7. Abusing parents sometimes have serious personality disorders. They may lack adequate impulse-control and get provoked easily.
8. Children vary in their temperaments; some are more difficult to rear than others. There may be a serious clash of temperaments between the child and parents. Some children find they only get parental attention when they behave in provocative ways, so that they apply patterns of behaviour which stimulate their parents to acts of violence, emotional abuse or incest.
9. Children with handicaps or disabilities of various sorts may be at an increased risk of abuse.

Effects

1. The susceptibility of a child to abuse and its health consequences are dependent upon the child's age and stage of development—the younger the child, more devastating the impact.
2. Abuse experiences, especially when they are multiple and prolonged, generally have a deleterious effect on the physical and mental well being of the child.
3. Abused children show anxiety and avoidance behaviour. They may become detached from their surroundings, and withdraw into a shell or manifest highly aggressive behaviour.
4. One of the common legacies of child abuse in any of its forms is a low self-esteem. Such children fail to achieve their potential in almost any of life's area.
5. Physical violence and sexual abuse in the home is a factor contributing to the phenomenon of 'street

children' in both developed and developing countries. Further abuse on the streets is an everyday reality.

Physical Abuse

Several children are brought to government hospitals or private health care facilities as a consequence of physical abuse (non-accidental injury) every year. About 5 to 10% of all children experience physical violence during childhood. According to some estimates one in 10,000 children under the age of five dies each year from physical violence.

Only rarely do families come asking for help because they are abusing their children. Suspected child abuse is sometimes reported to child welfare agencies by neighbours or relatives, who may have heard the child screaming in pain or have observed injuries. Other cases come to notice at school, in day care centers or during a visit to the doctor for some illness.

Few if any parents ever admit physically abusing their children. Many a time they come up with most improbable stories regarding their children's injuries. They may say that the child has fallen downstairs, out of bed or against an item of furniture or household appliance. The tales told by parents can be detailed and imaginative, but they are usually inconsistent and nearly always incompatible with the nature of the child's injuries. Moreover, a full and careful examination of the child generally reveals evidence of previous injuries.

Whatever the precipitating cause, it is the basic lack of parenting skills that leads to physical violence. Such parents are busy with their own life and instead of getting involved, neglect their children. When children seek attention they get irritated and resort to verbal and physical abuse. Severe shaking of a baby in a fit of rage or frustration may lead to bleeding inside the skull, due to tearing of blood vessels of the brain. This bleeding is slow and difficult to diagnose. If proper medical care is not made available quickly it can lead to brain damage or death.

The spectrum of injuries as a result of physical abuse is very wide. Starting from simple bruises and minor cuts it may extend to neurological damage and physical disability. The child who is brain damaged, mentally retarded, blind (retinal detachment) or deaf (damage to ear drum) as a result of physical violence is obviously at a disadvantage. Coupled with low self-esteem, these injuries can prevent the child from any worthwhile achievement.

Typical features of physical abuse

- There is generally a delay on the part of parents in seeking medical help.
- The explanation seems inadequate or incompatible with the injury.
- Previous suspicious injuries, equally unexplained, may be present in the child.
- The attitude of parents seems abnormal: indifferent or over-concerned.
- The parents may be reluctant to allow a full examination of the child.
- Bruising of the face, lips, mouth, eyes (black eye) or ears.

- Finger-shaped bruises.
- Small round burns (from cigarettes).
- Fracture of the skull, ribs and extremities.

Neglect

Child Abuse and Neglect (CAN) generally go hand in hand. Neglect is defined as, 'failing to provide proper care.' The earliest evidence of parental neglect is the 'failure to thrive' syndrome, where the child fails to grow and develop normally for no obvious medical reason. The weight and height of the child is below the expected normal for age. This growth retardation is accompanied by, developmental retardation and psychological symptoms such as listlessness and depression.

Why parents neglect their children? The commonest causes are the 'inability to respond to the needs of the child' or 'negative feelings towards the child.' Parents must respond promptly, consistently and correctly to the needs of their children. The role of mothers in the care of young babies can not be overemphasised. A mother suffering from depression or some other medical ailment may not be able to react in an appropriate, caring manner. Feeding time becomes a period of heightened stress, the baby cries excessively, takes too long to feed or vomits. Finally, the feeding problems become permanent and profound, resulting in failure of the infant to thrive.

It has been observed that mothers of children who fail to thrive show less pleasure in their babies, smile less, and spend less time talking and playing with them. This situation requires action at various levels:

- Telling the mother that "there is nothing wrong", merely adds to the problem.
- Provide emotional support to the mother. Psychotherapy may be contemplated in suitable cases.
- Nutritional advice and necessary medical treatment can help the baby grow optimally.

Emotional Abuse

As compared to physical and sexual, emotional abuse is harder to define and almost impossible to prove. What may be designated as abuse in one culture may be an acceptable child rearing practice in the other. Emotionally abused children suffer significant impairment of mental and emotional functioning. They may suffer from anxiety, depression, withdrawal or aggression. Compromised mental growth can lead to delayed development.

If children are repeatedly told that they are 'dumb,' 'stupid,' 'good for nothing' or 'retarded,' they are likely to believe what they are told, especially when it is the parents who utter these words. Once children develop the concept that they are worthless, it becomes a part of their self-image. It is little exaggeration to say that these children will end up as failures because from the very beginning they have been made to feel inferior.

Parents cause emotional injury by:

1. *Rejecting.* Parent refuse to look after the needs of the child and do not acknowledge his/her worth. This is an active form of neglect.
2. *Ignoring.* Here the parents fail to involve themselves in

the child's activities and deprive him/her of needed stimulation. Thus they subvert the child's emotional growth and intellectual development. This is a passive form of neglect.
3. *Taunting.* Inappropriate criticism, humiliation, ridicule or accusations can undermine a child's self-esteem and result in failures.
4. *Terrorising.* The child is verbally assaulted by the use of abusive language. Parents create an atmosphere of fear by the their malignant shouting and cursing. Constant threats make the child anxious and insecure and erode his/her self-image.
5. *Failing as role models.* Parents who are chronic alcoholics or drug abusers, or prone to domestic violence generally end up as social outcasts. They are perpetually in a financial mess and may suffer from stress, anxiety and various other psychological disorders. Tension prevalent in such homes stifles the child's personality.

Sexual Abuse

Sexual abuse of children and its impact on their psychosocial and intellectual growth has been the subject of increasing attention during the last two decades. Estimates of its prevalence may not be very accurate because the fear of social and legal implications lead to gross underreporting. Sexual abuse may be suspected if the child shows seductive behaviour, sexual knowledge inappropriate for his/her age or sexually precocious behaviour.

Sexual intercourse with a child by an older person is the extreme form of abuse, but 'inappropriate fondling' or 'dirty talk' also constitutes sexual abuse. Girls are the common victims and the perpetrators are generally family members or outsiders well known to the family. It may start when the child is quite young, even in the pre-school period and may continue for years. As the child grows and starts understanding relationships in their proper perspective, the enormity of what is happening dawns on her. She is faced with several distressing questions.

- Who should she tell?
- Will anyone believe her?
- Was it her fault?
- Will her family break if she tells?
- Will the abuser be punished or jailed?

The abuser may threaten the child with dire consequences if she ever tells anyone anything. He may also try to please her with gifts. He may tell her that they have a special relationship and that it is their own secret, to be shared with no one else. In her agony and confusion the child hesitates in disclosing the abuse and may never tell it to anyone.

Although there are several physical effects of sexual abuse like—rupture of hymen, tears and lacerations in vaginal and anal areas, sexually transmitted diseases and pregnancy, it is the psychological and emotional effects that are difficult to overcome. If it is a brief episode the child may overcome the trauma, but if it continues through much of childhood, the damage to child's psyche is more permanent.

The conflicts sexually abused children face are complex and agonizing. Their self-esteem suffers a serious damage, which leads to failures in many areas of life. The emotional consequences of abuse adversely affect their academic performance and their ability to form and maintain healthy relationships, especially with the opposite sex.

Sexually abused children suffer from feelings of guilt because they feel that it was, at least in part, their fault that abuse occurred. They may develop anger and hatred, directed primarily towards the abusing adult or towards the parent who failed to protect them or refused to believe them when told about the abuse. When these children try to suppress their anger they become frustrated and depressed and may develop suicidal tendencies. Sexually abused children may themselves become abusers of other children in later life.

Indicators of Sexual Abuse

Physical

- Presence of bruises, scratches and minor injuries in the genital area which are inconsistent with accident.
- Soreness, discharge and unexplained bleeding.
- The child may show signs of sexually transmitted diseases.
- Recurrent urinary tract infections.

Behavioural

- Sudden fluctuations in mood, anxiety and night terrors.
- Changes in eating or sleeping patterns.

- A child, who was previously dry by night, may start bedwetting.
- Attention seeking or disruptive behaviour.

It must be remembered that these physical and behavioural indicators may be present in conditions other than sexual abuse. No single indicator can be regarded as diagnostic, however, when dealing with a suspicious case these act as helpful clues.

Effect of Sexual Abuse

1. Low self-esteem.
2. Depression
3. Suicidal tendencies
4. Running away from home
5. Absenteeism from school.
6. Alcohol or drug abuse.
7. Promiscuity, compulsive masturbation
8. Physical violence
9. Delinquent and criminal behaviour.
10. Become child abusers themselves.

What can be done

- Teasing out the effects of specific abusive experiences is often difficult or impossible. The best option is to plan interventions that can prevent abuse from taking place.
- Understanding the developmental needs of children and adolescents and recognising their vulnerability to abuse, is as step in right direction.

- Promotion and support of the healthy development of children and adolescents is a prerequisite.
- Strengthening the capacity and resilience of the families is a necessity.

Child abuse is a social problem and each sector of the society has an important role to play in its prevention. There is a need for national programs for the prevention of child abuse, as well as for interventions that can help— the victims of child abuse and their families. Police, judicial authorities and others involved in investigating child abuse, particularly sexual abuse and exploitation need to be sensitive. They should be trained in methods for collection of information that do not cause more trauma and preserve the dignity of the child. While dealing with the families of abused children, a patient, painstaking and empathic approach is essential. These families tend to be especially defensive, as they are aware that they may face criminal charges and their children may be removed from their care.

Established or suspected child abuse should be reported to the appropriate authorities. It is usually better to deal with a responsible child welfare agency, the staff of which makes necessary liaison with the police. Once the abuse has come to light, the child welfare agency staff is responsible for the immediate welfare of the child; they must decide whether to remove the child from the care of the parents or guardians. Admission to hospital and medical or surgical treatment may be necessary. Meanwhile investigation of the family is carried out, usually by a social worker from the child welfare agency.

Abusive parents are frequently in need of psychiatric help; not only may they have established personality disorders, but they may be suffering from depression, anxiety disorders, alcoholism or the effects of drug abuse, all of which may respond to treatment. Individual psychotherapy may be needed for the abused children, especially when the abuse is of longstanding duration. Sometimes group therapy, in which children are treated along with others who have been similarly abused, proves more helpful than individual therapy.

The situation is different when a child has been abused by someone outside the family. In such cases the family is usually united in condemnation of the perpetrator and co-operates actively in the investigation and treatment of the case. At the same time there is an enormous emotional upheaval in the family; there may be guilt feelings on the part of the parents of allowing their child to be in a position to be abused. The parents may need guidance and help in dealing with the child and also with there own feelings.

For optimal growth and realisation of full potential children need warm, nurturing and affirming atmosphere of a stable, united family. A caring and supportive family environment can counter the potentially adverse effects of many traumatic and stressful experiences.

8

Illness can Undermine Self-esteem

Childhood is meant to bloom,
Not to wither away in gloom.

P.K.

Children suffering from physical illness, particularly chronic diseases and disabilities are at an obvious risk of developing low self-esteem. Illness can undermine a child's personality both directly and indirectly. Direct effects are ones, which result from the disability caused by the illness. Indirect effects of chronic illness my lead to a variety of personality disorders—low self-esteem being the commonest one.

Illness imposes limitations on the child's activities, especially if there is an associated physical disability. Chronically ill children or those having a physical handicap may view themselves as imperfect and different from their peers. They are likely to suffer from feelings of inferiority when they compare themselves with other children.

We live in a strange, prejudiced society which rejects sick and disabled children and looks down upon their families for giving birth to an imperfect child. Such is our apathy towards these children that many of us feel a sense of shame for having a chronically ill or imperfect child. We may never voice our disappointments at having a sick child, in fact most parents don't even consciously acknowledge it, but somehow the child becomes aware of it. What this does to the self-image of the affected child needs no illustration.

On one hand we have parents who neglect and reject their ill children, on the other there are some who suffer anxiety and guilt for giving birth to a sick/disabled child. Overprotective and anxious attitude of parents further retards the emotional development of children. These children face difficulties in social adjustments and may be subjected to teasing and bullying by their peers. Such children start avoiding school and are unable to concentrate on class work. Academic performance of sick children suffers on two count. Firstly, chronic illness may lead to repeated hospitalization or confinement to bed at home, thus children miss a lot of school and lag behind in the class. Secondly, such children may come to believe that because of their disease or disability they are less capable of achieving success as compared to their healthy peers. This may lead to academic and vocational failures in future.

Common Problems and their Effects

Asthma

Environmental pollution and asthma are two ugly facets of the same coin of development. The word asthma is derived from Greek and it means "breathless" or "to breathe with an open mouth". Childhood asthma cases have multiplied manifold in the last two decades. Asthma is a chronic respiratory disease, which, if not managed properly, can severely hamper the child's physical activities and academic performance. Unfortunately inspite of the availability of effective treatment, many children are forced to lead a compromised life. This happens because the lack of knowledge and information about childhood asthma either prevents the parents from seeking medical help or makes them hide the child's disease.

The reasons for increased prevalence of asthma may include changes in housing allowing greater proliferation of house dust mites, therefore increasing both sensitization and exposure. Environmental factors including both outdoor and indoor pollutants and changes in diet play an important role in the development of asthma. Impact of early childhood infections on the immune system (and therefore on allergy) is currently under investigation.

Precipitating Factors:

- Environmental factors: cold air, wind, fumes, dust, cigarette smoke and insecticides.
- Allergens.

- Viral infections.
- Allergy to fungus.
- Food additives and preservatives.
- Emotional stress.
- Exercise.
- Sinus disease.
- Drugs: aspirin, ibuprofen etc.

Children having asthma suffer from recurrent episodes of wheezing, breathlessness, chest tightness and cough, particularly at night and in early morning. Rapid respiration, anxiety and inability to complete sentences in one breath are usual accompaniments. These symptoms are due to widespread airflow limitation within the lungs. Often the attack is precipitated by a bout of respiratory infection. A family history of allergy like hay fever, asthma or eczema may be present in immediate relatives.

Children with poorly controlled asthma have a reduced ability to take part in games and other active pursuits. School absenteeism, lost sleep (because of nocturnal attacks) and growth retardation are the major problems affecting these children. As regards growth retardation, it is known that the growth hormone is produced in surges in sleep and during vigorous exercise. As these activities may be disrupted by uncontrolled asthma, this is perhaps the reason for growth retardation seen in asthmatic children.

Again, simple effective therapy will allow unrestricted exercise and will abolish night asthma, thus facilitating optimal growth.

Probably the most common question asked by parents of asthmatic children is: "will he/she grow out of it and if so, when?" There is no simple answer for this natural query. It has been observed that puberty tends to modulate symptoms and in about 70% of children the symptoms may lessen or disappear altogether after the age of eleven. Childhood asthmatics can be classified into two groups:

- Transient wheezers usually do not have symptoms by adolescence and may never develop asthma in adult life. If they smoke they might land up with asthma.
- Persistent wheezers tend to have symptoms in adolescence and go on to develop severe asthma in adult life.

The goal of asthma treatment is prevention of chronic and troublesome symptoms, thus enabling the child to lead a normal active life. Modern asthma therapy mainly relies on the use of various inhaled medications to control acute attacks and prevent recurrent exacerbation. Use of inhalers optimises the effect of drugs while at the same time minimizing the side effects. A wide variety of devices like rotahaler, spinhaler, metered-dose aerosol inhaler, spacer and nebuliser are readily available and within reach of most parents.

The problem of tackling a chronic disorder like asthma is not just a matter of clinical management, though this is important. In childhood it may be particularly difficult because of the child's parents, who are likely to feel guilty, and as a result of this may seek the elusive cure and not be satisfied with rational, effective therapy. Rogues promising complete cure of asthma abound in our country and try to exploit the worried parents. Fortunately, with adequate explanation, these problems are usually overcome.

It is essential that the patient and his/her family have a thorough understanding of the nature of asthma so that they understand the rationale of therapy and have realistic expectations. Till date there is no cure for asthma. But advances made in asthma research and treatment enables asthmatics to lead an absolutely normal life with complete control of the disease. Amitabh Bachchan, the greatest matinee idol, is an asthmatic but few non-asthmatics can ever hope to scale the heights achieved by him.

Epilepsy

Epilepsy is a common disabling condition, which has the potential not only to damage the brain but also self-esteem of the child. Inspite of treatment, epileptic fits do recur and can cause both physical and emotional trauma. Unfortunately, if the child gets a fit in the school, the reaction of classmates and teachers may vary from pity to outright rejection. In either situation, self-image of the child gets adversely affected.

In many societies, epilepsy is still associated with stigmas and taboos. Such children are abhorred, ridiculed and humiliated. They may suffer from feelings of shame at their plight. Parental anxiety gets communicated to them and they may start looking upon themselves as helpless and abnormal. When these feelings of hopelessness and defeat take root, self-esteem gets uprooted.

Parents tend to curtail the activities of their epileptic child. The arbitrary imposition of blanket embargoes on the things children like to do is not recommended. Pleasurable, well-motivated activity makes for a happy child and good seizure control.

Some Important Issues

- *Recreational Activities.* Swimming is permissible, especially when the seizure control is satisfactory and the child can be supervised by a competent swimmer. Cycling can be pursued safely in most children if seizures are well controlled but it is prudent to avoid cycling on busy roads. Children with epilepsy should be encouraged to participate in organised sports like football, hockey, cricket, basketball etc. Adventurous games like rock climbing and skating should be restricted. Dancing can be permitted although occasionally intermittent flashing lights might provoke an epileptic fit.
- *Travels and Excursions.* Epileptic children may become depressed and feel socially rejected if they are not allowed to go on a trip. The accompanying teachers should be told about the problem of the child and medicines that he/she has to take. First aid measures must also be explained.
- *Television and Video Games.* Some children get an epileptic fit by flickering lights. Only such children should be restricted from watching TV. For the rest of the epileptic children what is more important is to

avoid sleep deprivation and fatigue caused by endless hours of watching TV or playing video games.
- *Sleeping alone.* Many parents are terrified that their child will have a fit in sleep and may die in their sleep. It is advisable for one of the parents to sleep with the child in his/her room till epileptic fits are well controlled. Many parents allow a grown up epileptic child to sleep with them on a regular basis. This practice is to be discouraged because over-protection will almost certainly lead to development of inferiority complex in the child.
- *Gymnastics and Exercise.* Epileptic children can have regular exercise programs. In fact, these children are found to have fewer fits than children who lead a sedentary life.
- *School.* Children with epilepsy are educationally vulnerable because of a variety of reasons:
  – Poor control of seizures.
  – Side effects of anti-epileptic medications.
  – Rejection, ridicule or pity of peers and teachers.

Most children with epilepsy are able to attend regular schools. Teachers and school management should be informed of the child's condition because hiding the diagnosis may actually harm the child by depriving him/her of the much-needed psychological support.

Do's and Don'ts

- Avoid seizure-precipitating factors: e.g. sleep deprivation, constipation, extreme hunger and fatigue, bright flickering light etc.

- Regular and timely administration of prescribed drugs is an absolute must. Highly effective and relatively safe anti-epileptic drugs are now available.
- Avoid sudden stoppage of anti-epileptic drugs.
- TV should be watched from at least 2 meters in a well-illuminated room.
- Use sunglasses when going outdoors.
- During an attack keep the child on his/her side and wipe away the froth from mouth to help breathing. Do not place anything in the mouth to "prevent the tongue being bitten", as it can choke the child.
- Blankets, sheets and extra clothing should not be applied.

Obesity

Several studies have demonstrated that obese children are at a high risk to develop diabetes, hypertension, heart disease and arthritis in later life. Surely the future appears bleak, but the present isn't pleasant either. Obese children are often the butt of jokes and face insult and isolation.

Childhood obesity is a challenging problem, which is on the rise not only in the western world, but also in a developing nation like India. Approximately 10-15% children between 6-18 years of age are obese. Childhood obesity is a well-established risk factor for obesity in adulthood: 80% of obese children are expected to remain obese as adults.

The causes of obesity are complex and multiple. Basically, obesity occurs when an individual consumes more calories than the body burns up. Genetic factor plays an important role in the development of obesity. Obese parents get obese children. If one parent is obese, there is a 50% chance of the child being fat. There are several hormonal and neurological disorders, which are associated with obesity.

Sedentary life style and intake of high fat, high calorie foods and snacks is largely responsible for the development of obesity. The advent of television has contributed to this menace in a big way. It has been observed that prevalence of obesity increases by 2% for every hour of TV viewing. With more and more children playing games on computers rather than on the field the incidence of obesity is bound to increase. Dependence on automobiles for transport is growing at an alarming rate amongst adolescents and is sure to compound the problem of obesity.

Management of Obesity

Childhood obesity is a great challenge for the pediatrician and prevention appears to be the only tool in fighting this scourge. Diet, exercise and behaviour modifications are the mainstays of therapy. Appetite-suppressing drugs are not recommended in children and adolescents because they may adversely affect the growth of the child.

Diet: Educating parents and the children regarding proper nutrition is of utmost importance. Energy-dense, high fat, high calorie snacks and fast foods and sweetened aerated beverages must be cut down drastically if any substantial reduction in weight is to be achieved. These should be replaced with fruits (excluding bananas), vegetables, lentils etc. A balanced hypo-calorie diet, which gives 1200-1800 calories per day (or a deficit of around 40% of usual intake) and is low in fat, with high fibber content is recommended for obese children. This allows the children to lose weight gradually (0.5 kg/week) but lets them grow normally.

Exercise: Lack of exercise and sedentary life style causes more weight gain in children as compared to adults. Children should be motivated to take up cycling, aerobics, cricket, basketball, football, badminton etc. They will enjoy these activities and are likely to continue with them. Rigorous, monotonous exercise will annoy and frustrate children, with a negative impact on the final outcome. Parents and teachers should try to strike a balance between after-school academic pursuits and out-door physical activities.

Behaviour Modification

- Try to identify and analyse the child's problems. Entire family, along with the pediatrician should be involved in this process.
- Set realistic goals and try to achieve them by maintaining a 'DIET DIARY' and an 'EXERCISE LOG'.
- Obtain information regarding calories and nutritive value of common foods from your doctor.
- Develop a daily exercise schedule.
- Limit TV watching, computer time etc.
- Do not stuff the fridge with goodies. Parents must set an example by not eating food forbidden for the child.

- Encouragement and rewards for good performance by the child are highly effective.
- Build child's self-confidence and self-esteem by having a sensitive and positive attitude towards his/her needs.

Visual and Auditory Impairment

Children who use spectacles or hearing aids are teased by their peers. They are faced with a daunting task of overcoming not only their disability but also the negative attitude of others. More than the disability it is the prejudice of society that can seriously damage their pride.

Refractive errors of varying degree and severity are quite common in childhood. A myopic child may not be able to see the blackboard clearly and this may lead to poor academic performance. Visual defects are the commonest cause of headache in children and can be easily managed by use of proper glasses. With the advent of computerised refraction, the procedure of eye testing and correction in children has become simplified and fast.

If the spectacle lenses are thick and unwieldy, contact lenses are now available. Present day soft contact lenses are of good quality and do not cause eye irritation. LASIK technique (laser treatment) has ushered in a new era in the treatment of refractive errors and eliminated even the use of contact lenses. Vision obtained through contact lenses or after LASIK is of better quality than spectacle lenses.

The presence of squint in a child is of serious importance. These children are devoid of binocular vision and the eye affected by squint nearly always has subnormal vision. Additionally, the constant teasing, ridicule and derogatory remarks of peers can adversely affect the psyche of these children. Squint can be easily corrected by surgery and good cosmetic effect and near normal vision is usually obtained by most children.

Presence of hearing impairment should be seriously attended to. Highly effective and cosmetically acceptable hearing devices are now readily available. Audiometry can detect even minor hearing defects and the use of proper hearing aid can help the child socially as well as academically.

Acne

Acne is the most common skin problem of the adolescent years, and majority of teenagers at some stage suffer from varying degrees of acne. The impact of acne on the teenagers may be enormous. Adolescents dislike all blemishes; they may feel that the problem of acne is adversely affecting their popularity and interpersonal relationships at a time of life when these are of extreme importance to them.

Adolescents suffering from acne may or may not seek help but it should be borne in mind that they need and must be provided careful attention. To tell them that treatment is unnecessary and the disease will disappear spontaneously at the end of adolescence is not fair to them, because treatment can prevent scarring. The scars of acne are known to damage the face and psyche in equal proportions.

Management

The face should be washed with mild soap and water at least twice daily. Vigorous scrubbing is not recommended as it does more harm than good. Steaming the face for 2-3 minutes once a week is useful in acne patients. Ointments and creams containing benzoyl peroxide, erythromycin or clindamycin are helpful in controlling acne. These should be applied on the entire acne prone area. Avoid exposure to sun. Treatment should be continued for six months or more. Acne extraction with an extractor is useful. Oral antibiotics are reserved for more severe and resistant cases. Doxycycline 100mg daily for 1-2 months is the most commonly used drug.

Skin pigmentation and scarring resulting from acne is extremely traumatic both physically and emotionally for an adolescent. Various surgical techniques like chemical peeling and micro-dermabrasion can improve the appearance by reducing pigmentation and superficial scarring. A number of sittings are required, hence patience is the key to the success of treatment.

Myths and Realities regarding Skin Care

Myths	Realities
Oily and spicy food leads to the development of acne	It has been conclusively proved that food has no relation to the problem of acne.
Household cosmetics are harmless.	They can cause irritation, redness, skin allergies and may increase the acne production

Myths	Realities
Cleansing milks and face packs are more effective in cleaning the deep pores.	They offer no advantage over soaps.
Regular steaming is good for skin.	Too frequent steaming leaves large open pores and may lead to premature ageing of skin.
Skin creams and moisturisers with vitamin A, E etc. improve the skin condition.	Most of these are not absorbed and have no added advantage.

Bed Wetting

Bedwetting or enuresis is a common childhood problem in which there is an involuntary passage of urine during sleep. It is frequent cause of emotional turmoil and tension in several homes. Children with the problem of bedwetting suffer from low self-esteem, shame and guilt. They are afraid of being discovered by their peers and often fear being teased and humiliated by their own siblings and relatives. They opt out of social activities. Most bedwetting children will not go to camps or participate in sleepovers with friends.

Children should not be labeled 'bedwetters' unless the symptoms persist beyond the age of five years. There is little justification for starting drug treatment before this age as most of the times the child becomes all right by this time. Bedwetting occurs more frequently in boys than in girls. It will often have been present in one of the parents. Bedwetting is broadly divided into two types:

Persistent type

In this type the child has never been dry at night. It is often due to faulty toilet training. If the parents are very rigid, it may lead to an angry response from the child. The child may unconsciously defy the parents by wetting the bed. On the other hand if parents are not supportive and sufficiently involved in toilet training, the child will fail to develop good bladder control, leading to his/her wetting the bed.

Regressive type

In this type a child who was previously dry at nights begins to wet the bed at night, after a stressful episode. Move to a new house, marital conflict, sexual abuse, birth of a sibling, death in the family, school-related stress all are capable of inducing bedwetting. This type of bedwetting is often intermittent and transitory; prognosis is better and management is less difficult than in those children who have never been dry.

In both types of bedwetting, generally no physical abnormality is found. A urine examination should be routinely done in all bedwetting children to exclude urinary tract infection. When bedwetting is associated with urinary infection, treatment of the infection promptly cures the problem.

Management

Bedwetting is a perplexing problem to manage. The best results are achieved when a child is motivated, there is close co-operation between child, parents and the doctor and there is no evidence of serious psychiatric problem in the child or family.

General Measures

- Rewarding the child for being dry at night is a useful step. The child feels encouraged and is likely to make a sincere effort to avoid passing urine in bed.
- Punishment or humiliation of the child by parents or others should be strongly discouraged. The child is likely to lose confidence and may even develop defiance, leading to aggravation of the problem.
- In case of young children the parents should change the soiled clothes. Older children should be expected to wash the clothes soiled by them. But this should not be turned into a prestige issue by the parents.
- Children should be given no liquids after dinnertime.
- The child should be asked to pass urine before going to bed.
- Parents may wake up the child once, to take him/her to bathroom, when they are retiring to bed. Waking the child repeatedly to pass urine is not advised as it may provoke anger and resentment in the child.

Enuresis Alarm

In western countries various alarm systems are available. These rely on a sensor placed under the sheets, which detects the passage of a small amount of urine and sets off an alarm to wake the child. Enuresis alarm is a simple, safe and effective device for bedwetting. The principle behind using these alarms is, to awaken the children when they are bedwetting, by an external alarm system, until they learn to recognise their own internal signal of bladder fullness while in deep sleep, and awaken on their own to empty the bladder.

Drugs

The most effective drug in the treatment of bedwetting is Imipramine. This medication has, however some side effects and should only be used under close medical supervision. Many children start bedwetting again after stopping this drug. Two other drugs Amantidine and Oxybutinin have also been tried with varying degree of success.

An ayurvedic preparation 'Mentat' has been claimed to be effective in the treatment of bedwetting. Precise scientific data supporting these claims is not available. Also, the exact mechanism of action of this medication is not known.

Recently an entirely new modality of treatment for bedwetting has become available. This comes in the form of nasal spray and nasal drops, which are to be instilled in the nose of the child at bedtime. It contains desmopressin hormone (Minrin, Dvoid) which reduces the urinary output, thus providing quick relief from bedwetting. The cost of the treatment with this drug is around Rs.1000/- per month.

To summarise, bedwetting is a multi-factorial problem, which requires a multidisciplinary approach. With proper management the results are generally good.

Stammering or stuttering

Stammering is an important psychosomatic condition, which may be a cause or an effect of inferiority complex. A child who stammers in class falls prey to constant teasing and ridicule by peers and even teachers. Mishandling on the part of parents can compound the problem. The child may keep stammering and stuttering throughout his/her life and fail in one endeavour after another.

Stammering is the repeated interruption of the flow of speech by repetition, prolongation or blocking of sounds. In children aged 2 to 4 there are often hesitations, repetitions of the first sounds of words or phrases and irregularities in the rhythm of speech. The less emphasis paid to this early stammering, the better the outcome. During this phase, the condition generally resolves spontaneously if child is not made conscious by over anxious parents. The child can be made to feel successful and cared for in other areas. This helps the child overcome the problem within a short time.

Persistent stammering has a familial predisposition, and is more common in boys than girls. Disturbed parent-child relationship, anxiety and stress aggravate the problem. The causes of stammering are not fully understood. For instance, some stammerers can sing fluently or speak normally while acting on stage but stammer in ordinary conversation. Some children speak fluently at home but stammer at school. Some are worse when anxious, while others are not.

The severity of stammering varies from occasional repetition of speech sounds to severe blocking of speech. When these children try to speak there is a spasm of the speech muscles i.e. lips, throat, larynx, and the speech is entirely blocked.

Stammering can drastically affect a child's life. Failure to communicate properly leads to the development of avoidance behaviour which ultimately turns into a full-blown inferiority complex. Poor academic achievement may be a direct consequence of the inability to speak normally or it may be the result of low self-esteem.

Management

No treatment is generally required for early stammering but speech therapy is essential in cases of persistent stammering. Specific techniques such as *syllabic speech* may be used; stammerers are taught, usually in a group setting, to speak slowly and deliberately, syllable by syllable. Breath control exercises may help some children. Use of a miniaturised metronome that "paces" the rhythm of speech, is also recommended by therapists.

Psychotherapy should be reserved for cases in which there is associated emotional disorder in child or family. Techniques designed to relive anxiety, promote relaxation and encourage self-confidence may help. Hypnosis and hypnotherapy may be useful adjunct in the treatment of stammering.

Constitutional Differences

Each child grows and matures at his/her own pace. A girl who develops breast buds at nine or the one whose first period only arrives at fifteen are as normal as their peer group whose breast development and first period starts around the average age of twelve years. Very often, asymmetrical breast development—which is quite common initially, can be extremely distressing to both mother and child. Similarly absence of genital hair and penile size or shape are a frequent cause of worry among boys. Pubertal breast enlargement sometimes becomes a bothersome issue and a source of acute embarrassment to the boy and his family. I have examined several adolescent boys with gynaecomastia (breast enlargement) who were suffering from extreme anxiety and feelings of low self-esteem. In all of them the problem resolved on its own with passage of time.

There are a number of constitutional differences in growth parameters, which can cause acute anxiety in children and result in the development of inferiority complex. Many of these problems come to light during sports and other co-curricular activities at school. This leads to self-isolation and can affect all other areas of development. Most of these cases only need reassurance that in time these problems will get solved automatically, as the hormonal changes finally settle down.

Miscellaneous Conditions.

Malodor is a peculiar problem in some children and may lead to shunning by peers. Foul smell coming from the mouth must be treated promptly as it denotes infection. Puberty goiter is a common medical problem seen in adolescents during the phase of rapid physical growth. It appears as a midline swelling in the front of the neck and is due to the enlarged thyroid gland. During pubertal growth spurt, the need of thyroid hormone increases. To meet this increased demand there is a compensatory enlargement of the thyroid gland. Usually at the end of puberty this thyroid enlargement disappears on its own, but in some cases, especially when the swelling persists after the age of 18 years, medical treatment may be necessary.

Several other medical conditions predispose the child to the development of inferiority complex. Cleft lip, deformities of limbs and spine, short stature all can undermine a child's personality. Congenital cardiac diseases (hole in the heart), metabolic disorders (juvenile diabetes), hormonal deficiencies (hypothyroidism) etc. may prevent the child from achieving his/her potential.

Dealing with Sick Children

Acquisition of self-confidence, emotional stability and a capacity to think rationally are the most important developmental tasks of childhood. If this process of psychological maturation is compromised due to illness, the child is unable to deal with life's challenges and frustrations in a balanced way. He/she will not be able to function satisfactorily leading to maladjustment and failure.

An apparently highly intelligent and talented child may fail in life because of his/her illness. Generally this failure is not entirely due to illness itself, psychological trauma caused by the disease also plays a significant role. The condescending attitude of parents and teachers, rejection by peers and the child's own feelings of inadequacy and imperfection can lead to the development of inferiority complex.

Personality and temperament are greatly influenced by environmental factors, but genes also contribute powerfully. This makes some children more resilient than others in coping with illness. It is indeed a fact that many children with disabilities develop compensatory strengths in unaffected areas. Thus the hearing of a blind child may become particularly acute or a child suffering from a physical disability, which prevents his/her participation in outdoor activities, may excel in studies.

Illness has the potential to affect a child's self-esteem adversely. Whether the child fails or succeeds in life depends upon the attitudes of parents, teachers and other persons in close contact with the child. It is much better to concentrate on the talents, strengths and success that the child displays. Treating the child as 'normal' rather than as 'sick' is generally a preferred option. However this should not be overdone, otherwise inadvertently the child may be denied needed health care and educational and emotional support.

9

Combating Inferiority Complex

No one can make you feel inferior without your consent.
                                                    Eleanor Roosevelt.

Inferiority complex or low self-esteem is variously defined as—poor self-image, feeling of worthlessness, sense of insecurity, state of self-doubt, timidity and so on. It is a major hurdle in the path to success and glory, and can become a stumbling block for many a potential winners.

High self-esteem is feeling good about oneself, knowing one's strengths and weaknesses, accepting them and acting in accordance with them. However, it should not be confused with an inflated ego, which is the prime reason behind the premature demise of many promising careers.

Success and self-esteem have a close and direct relationship. Success is important for the growth of positive feeling about oneself and affirmation of worth. A child with high self-esteem can use a failure as a learning experience while a child with low self-esteem gets bogged down. We experience 'lows' and 'highs'. On some days we feel more confident, on others we are down in the dumps. Feeling less sure and suffering from doubts from time to time is all right, but persistent feelings of worthlessness and insecurity are a matter of grave concern.

Children with high self-esteem are able to express their feelings and emotions in a controlled manner. They generally succeed in influencing other people's behaviour in a positive way. These children approach new challenges with confidence and show a lot of independence and responsibility. They don't get easily frustrated by failures, and view them in proper perspective. Through persistence and perseverance they turn failures into resounding success. Children with high self-esteem are full of ideas and are able to control their environment through their positive approach.

Children with low self-esteem are low on confidence and generally speak in self-derogatory terms. They go on the defensive easily and avoid situations which may cause confrontation and tension. They are unable to form opinions and rely on other's judgement. To counter doubts about self they constantly blame others for their problems and failures. They are not open to reason and feel powerless when faced with any challenging situation. They avoid new experiences and shy away from interactions. Children with low-esteem have low frustration tolerance; thus they tend to give up without putting in a worthwhile effort. These children use the crutches of fate and luck to plod along an ill-defined path that leads nowhere.

The 'How' and 'Why' of Inferiority Complex

Every child is born—a winner, but whether he/she will succeed in later life depends upon a complex interplay of several related factors. Children develop positive personalities only if they are encouraged by people and circumstances which ensure that their self-esteem is carefully nourished throughout the crucial growing-up years. Genetic endowment or the potential to succeed may be present but it can be blocked by adverse environmental factors operating at home, at school and in society. When this happens, it results in a collapse of confidence and withdrawal from the struggle towards worthwhile achievement.

Predisposing Factors

(A) Faulty Parental Attitudes

1. Lack of communication
2. Rejection
3. Harsh discipline
4. Unrealistic demands
5. Undue comparison
6. Overprotection

(B) Dysfunctional Family Situation

1. Parental discord
2. Separation/Divorce
3. Death in the family
4. Frequently moving family
5. Parent's loss of job
6. Parent's unhealthy addiction

(C) Maladjustment At School

1. Peer pressure
2. Peer rejection
3. Punitive teachers
4. Style of teacher versus style of student
5. Language difficulties
6. Slow learner

(D) Others

1. Sibling performance
2. Health related problems e.g. Asthma, Obesity
3. Abuse
4. Learning disabilities
5. Traumatic emotional development
6. Odd surname, dark complexion, use of spectacles etc.

Timid, anxious children lacking in confidence, despite their superior intelligence, generally underachieve. They are unable to realise their potential and regard themselves as failures. This further undermines their confidence and damages their self-esteem. Thus a vicious circle in formed which is difficult to break.

The Vicious Cycle of Inferiority Complex

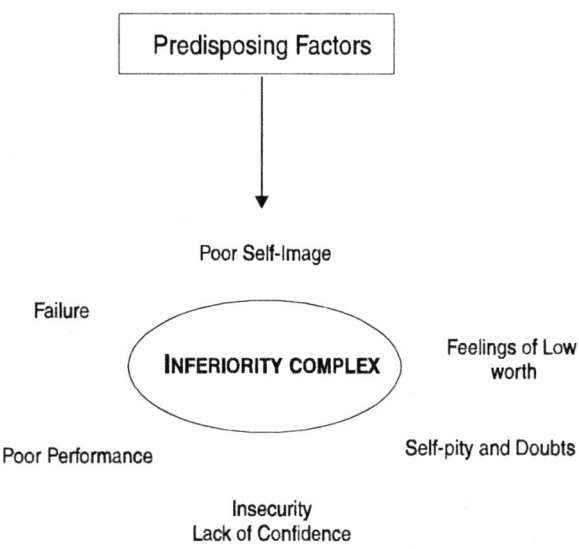

"It is important for us to listen to what children feel and want for their world."

Rippan Kapur.

Parents who do not communicate and interact with their children deprive them of the knowledge, experience and wisdom they have acquired over the years. Lack of communication has the potential to undermine a child's personality and lower his/her aspirations.

Probably the commonest comment made by teachers in the report cards of children is—'could do better'. Much is made of the child's inability to cope with examinations by many teachers and parents. Constant reminders to the child at school and home that he/she is careless and does not work hard enough can only make the child lose heart and create doubts about self.

Some parents put excessive pressure on their children through their unrealistic demands. If children fail to measure up to the parental expectations they lose faith in their abilities. Repeated failures erode self-confidence, and gradually the child develops a maladjusted personality burdened with low self-esteem.

Undue comparison is a potent weapon in the hands of parents by which they can cause serious and permanent damage to the child's self-esteem. Parents keep citing the example of children who are brilliant in studies and outstanding in sports. They do this in the hope of motivating their children to perform better, but it generally has an opposite effect. Mostly the child's performance worsens. There can be two reasons for this—firstly, the child under-performs deliberately to show his/her revolt against the parental dictates. The child resents praise for peers, especially when it comes from his/her parents. Secondly, the child may be genuinely incapable of living up to the parents' high expectations. Thus, unnecessary and unjustified comparisons can only harm the child's self-image.

Faulty discipline and low self-esteem have a symbiotic relationship—both thrive together. Whether it is excessively harsh, inconsistent or over-permissive—flawed discipline will harm the child's personality. It has been observed that in the long run, punishment is an ineffectual technique for eliminating the kind of behaviour against which it is directed. Punishment tends to orient the child away from reality, and makes him/her insecure and more dependent upon adult affection and attention. Effective use of discipline is the key to successful adjustments in life.

Many children develop profound worries relating to persistent parental discord. They fear that this will lead to divorce and abandonment. Generally these anxieties are not based on reality but may be due to comparisons with classmates from so-called 'broken-homes' or a direct consequence of the innumerable 'family-soaps' shown on the idiot box. Parental illness or unemployment and financial hardship can also prevent all round personality development of the child.

Anxiety due to any cause can adversely affect self-image. Anxious children are self-depreciating, low on confidence and unable to face day to day challenges. They also tend to be low in curiosity and adventurousness and while away their time daydreaming. These children are taunted by peers and scorned by teachers. With such an all-encompassing negative environment it is not difficult to understand why these children get trapped in the vicious cycle of inferiority complex.

Parental messages are deeply ingrained in children's minds and have a potent effect on their future scholastic achievement and social adjustments. If children are repeatedly told that they are no good, they presume it to be a true evaluation of their worth. Gradually the feeling of inferiority takes root and these children start believing that they are worthless.

Seven Steps to Building Self-esteem

One of the most precious gifts you can give your child is a sense of self-worth. For accomplishing this, you must first evaluate your own feelings of self-esteem. If you suffer from feelings of inadequacy you will find it extremely difficult to help your child. You must believe in yourself, have faith in your child's capabilities and view things positively.

The following recommendations to improve your child's self-esteem should be applied with consistency and discretion. It must be remembered that no single suggestion by itself can make a significant impact. Moreover, several other factors not within your control, such as peer pressure, teacher's attitudes etc. will also affect the child's self-esteem. However, your genuine desire to help your child will ultimately decide his/her fate.

Find Solutions, not Faults

Are you quick to point a finger if your child makes a mistake? Do you constantly criticise the child for his/her behaviour? If yes, then you are sending wrong messages to your child. Parents who merely blame the child for his/her faults and fail to teach correct behaviour, cause irreparable damage to their child's self-esteem. These children never learn to handle difficult situations and get easily frustrated and disheartened.

Instead of finding faults parents should be busy fixing them. They should try to ensure that the mistake and misbehaviour do not recur, and give children the opportunity to realise and analyse their mistakes. This makes them more responsible and resilient and gradually they learn right behaviour and develop right attitudes.

Use Rewards, Avoid Punishment

Rewards reinforce desired behaviour, while punishment strengthens feelings of worthlessness. All children want to win parental approval. Some make it quite obvious by their continuous efforts; others project an indifferent exterior, but may work towards gaining parental praise in their own private way. The onus of reconising, appreciating and rewarding children's efforts lies on the parents.

Throughout this book I have repeatedly advocated the use of reward system in the hope that parents will adopt it and use it more often. Rewards need not always be monetary or in the form of gifts. Praise, show of affection or a pat on the back works equally well and is quite effective in generating feeling of self-worth.

Let Children take Decisions

The ability to think clearly and decide quickly is the hallmark of all successful people. Allowing children to take decisions that affect their daily life gives them an opportunity to exercise self-control and enhances their self-esteem. It also makes them more adept at taking major decisions in later life. Decisions about clothes to wear, toothpaste or soap to use, photographs to decorate own room, friends to invite to the birthday party, selecting the menu—all can help the child grow in confidence. Mistakes are bound to happen but they must be viewed positively and utilised as learning experiences.

Don't Handle Kids with 'Kid Gloves'

Each time you rush to the aid of your children you underline their incompetence and undermine their confidence. Unwittingly you are reinforcing feelings of low self-esteem. Some parents have the tendency to 'bail-out' their children each time they are confronted with a difficult situation. To prevent children from facing frustration and possible failure parents try to alter the environment, in an attempt to make it more favourable. In shielding children from every danger, such parents deny them opportunities for reality testing. These children get a distorted view of the world and may become so dependent that they are unable to meet any challenge without adult help.

The ability to master the environment and find solutions to problems is crucial to the development of a positive self-image. Isadora Duncan said, **"The finest inheritance you can give a child is to allow it to make its own way completely on its own feet."** Parents must allow children to explore and experiment. When children are permitted to profit from their own mistakes with a minimum of adult interference they tend to be more confident, less dependent on adults and capable of facing reality. These children have high self-esteem and strong feelings of self-worth.

Leave Scope for Disagreement

We live in a democratic society, which bestows on us the freedom of speech. As adults we have the independence to agree or disagree with any viewpoint. Should our children be denied this basic right?

Children must be given opportunities to express themselves and register their protests. Parents and teachers should be prepared to listen to children's point of view. Even when their point of view does not evoke a favourable response, the knowledge that they were given a sympathetic and sincere audience, makes children feel important and worthy. Such opportunities convince children that they have a say in matters concerning them. They come to realise that they have the power to change their environment and mould their destiny.

Allow Success to Succeed

Once a child successfully accomplishes a task provide him/her with more opportunities to do it again. With repeated opportunity and success, the child masters the required skills and develops confidence. Simple tasks such as making tea, boiling eggs, taking telephone messages, fixing something around the house, making the shopping list can be used to repeat success. Proven track of success is the ultimate proof of high self-esteem.

Set Realistic Goals

Setting realistic goals and helping children achieve them is an important factor in improving self-esteem. Left to themselves children may set unrealistic goals, fail to achieve them and lose confidence. When this happens they become unwilling to venture out and face new challenges. Such children become limited in their experience and are vulnerable to failure. Repeated failures lead to development of avoidance behaviour and feelings of inferiority.

You must help your children in deciding their priorities and defining their goals. Once you know what the child wants to achieve, prepare a time bound program to go about it. Define clearly the steps necessary to reach the goal and treat each step as a smaller goal. If the child gets stuck at any stage offer him/her alternative ways to accomplish the task. Slowly but surely your child will reach the top with feelings of accomplishment at every step.

Words to Omit

Parents who want to improve their child's self-esteem must omit the following seven words from their dictionary:

- Criticism
- Hostility
- Ridicule
- Rejection
- Disapproval
- Discouragement
- Unfairness

10

All Children Have Fears

I hope when I become an adult I will not forget I was ever a child.

Mitesh P.

Humans thrive on emotions. Love, passion, fervour, joy, grief, pathos, anger, hate, wrath, fear, valour—all are an essential part of the collage called 'life'. Every child goes through the normal stages of emotional development. If the conditions are favourable he/she develops into an emotionally secure, confident adult.

All children have fears. Parents should not get distressed or overtly worried by their child's fears, otherwise inadvertently they will heighten their dread and worsen the situation. Certain fears are 'age-appropriate', and only when the child fails to overcome them in due course of time, active intervention should be contemplated.

Some parents refuse to acknowledge and accept children's fears as a natural part of growing up. They feel that there is something wrong with a fearful child. Their refusal to admit the child's fears as real makes them appear unkind but the truth is, somewhere deep down they have a perception of failing as parents.

Fear is the key to survival. It is a 'protective' emotion, which induces us to take precautions, to be wary, watchful, circumspect and prudent. The fear of falling from roof keeps us away from the parapet. We take care while crossing the road. We carry a torch when we go out in the dark—thus fear helps us minimise risks.

Fear is an universal emotion present in and manifested by all living things. Because of their superior brain and greater sensibility human beings respond to a vast spectrum of threatening stimuli. A child's fears actually aren't much different from those of an adult. But grown-ups have the advantage of experience on their side. They have learnt to handle intimidating situations; children have not. Children are yet to master the emotion of fear.

Normal Fears: As the child goes through various stages of emotional development certain fears are quite normal. The fear of falling and sudden loud sound is innate to all human babies. If a baby is suspended face down supported on the palm, and the palm is suddenly brought down, the baby extends its arms and legs as if to break the fall. This is also known as the 'parachute reflex' and is a protective response against falling. Similarly young babies also show 'startle response' to any sudden loud noise. They move their limbs and body in sudden jerky movements and take a few moments before calming down. This reaction is sustained even in adult life, albeit in a toned down manner.

Around six months of age children can be expected to be afraid of strangers. They are now able to recognise their family members and feel threatened by unfamiliar faces. Strangers represent a potential threat to their security and survival.

At about ten months the fear of being abandoned develops and is strongest between the ages of one and two. Whenever the mother goes out of sight for some time, the child feels that she has gone forever. This causes intense anxiety, which is relieved only when she returns. During this stage parents should avoid prolonged or frequent separation from the child. Gradually the child learns to cope with the disappearances of parents and develops a sense of security.

Fear of dark predominates around two to three years of age but may extend well beyond childhood. Even adults fear night because darkness is associated with thefts, murders and other dangerous things. As children enter their teenage years, the concept of death becomes clear to them. They experience the greatest anxiety about the death of a parent. Several children develop fear of going blind or contracting some other fatal illness.

Nightmares: It is quite common for children to experience nightmares between 3-6 years of age. The exact reason is not known, but it is believed that they are related to the normal anxiety and stress that are a part of growing children's lives.

During a nightmare the child needs his/her parent's comfort and support. Get to the child as quickly as possible and once there stay with the child till he/she overcomes the nightmare and falls back into his/her normal sleep cycle. Keep comforting the child by gently stroking his/her head for some time. Many children remember their dreams the next day. Encourage them to talk about their dreams in the morning. Discuss and suggest ways to overcome the things in the dream that were frightening.

When a Child Gets Lost: Inspite of a parent's best precautions children do manage to lose themselves. Generally, parents can't be faulted for these mishaps. Agreed, some parents are careless, but not to the extent of risking losing the children.

When children get lost—in a busy market or a fair, and remain separated from their parent for a substantial length of time, they develop acute anxiety and may acquire a permanent fear of being lost. These children are afraid of venturing out alone and mostly stick to the side of their parents or other adults known to them.

Such children show excessive separation anxiety at the time of beginning school and may fail to establish meaningful relationships with peers and teachers. While dealing with these children parents and teachers must accept their fear as a natural consequence of the traumatic experience of being lost. With assurance gradually most children overcome their fear and gain confidence.

Television Violence: Children these days are exposed to several experiences causing anxieties—television violence being one of the major culprits. **Tushar**, nine, was a well-adjusted, bright and happy child. He was perfectly comfortable sleeping in his room, adjacent to his parents.' One evening while his parents were away he saw a TV program on a serial child killer. He couldn't sleep in the night because of fear and kept a vigil for the murderer. When the light in his parents room was switched off he quietly slipped inside and slept on the floor.

Tushar was so upset by the horror scenes shown on the program that he lost the courage to sleep alone in his bedroom. Night after night, he started creeping into his parents' bed. His parents were also greatly disturbed by this new development.

'Barrier Parenting' may seem a new and fancy coinage but is essentially an old, time trusted practice. Parents must actively monitor whether the things going into the child's mind are healthy or unhealthy. Tushar's parents need to discuss the problem with him and reassure him. They should let him sleep with them—legally—for some time. They must also plan happy experiences to fill his mind. Gradually, over the next days they can make him sleep in his room keeping the night-lamp on and the interconnecting door open.

Show them the Way: Children model their behaviour by observing their parents. Parents, who deal confidently with situations which children find intimidating, set a positive example.

During an orthodontic check-up of my daughter, the dentist advised removal of four teeth to achieve proper alignment. Naturally, she was terrified! Even I am petrified by the sight of dental instruments. I had been postponing the removal of an impacted tooth for years. I decided to set an example and steeled myself for the assault of stainless steel dental pliers.

A few days later my daughter accompanied me to the dentist's clinic and observed my dental extraction pass off smoothly. My calm, composed (and calculated) response helped her gain confidence and gather courage. She completed her orthodontic treatment without much fuss. Actually, the pluck she showed during all those extractions was quite remarkable.

It is not necessary to act courageous at all times, sometimes it helps to admit fear. When you tell your children that you too used to be afraid of the dark, they will realise they aren't alone in feeling scared. By seeing that you no longer fear darkness, they will learn an important lesson—fears can be mastered.

Never Terrorise a Child: We carry the fears and misgivings of childhood into our adult life. Frightening a child with a lizard or a bearded man can instil a permanent fear in his/her mind. Such a child withdraws from his environment, becomes a recluse and lacks confidence. He/she may lose heart easily and give up without putting up a fight. This child can develop a variety of complexes.

It has been observed that up to the age of three years, the emotion of fear is not deep rooted and can be easily removed by the active involvement of parents. But around five years, fear leaves a strong impact on the child's mind and teasing out its effect becomes much more difficult.

When you terroise your child by saying: "if you don't study the lion will eat you", you create a dread in the child's mind. Later if you take him/her to a zoo or a circus, he/she will be terror-struck at the sight of the lion. Thus, what should have been a happy outing, becomes an embarrassment for you and a nightmare for your child.

Parents use fear as a convenient tool to control their children.

- If you don't eat food bogeyman will take you away.
- If you don't stop crying we will give you to the policeman.
- If you don't drink milk we will ask the doctor to fill in his syringe and inject it in your tummy.

Most of the children coming to my clinic have been threatened practically every day by their parents for something or the other. When nothing seems to work they use the ultimate threat—"Wait! We will take you to Dr. Kapoor's Clinic for an injection." With the result that when these children enter my clinic, they expect me to pounce on them with an injection in my hand. This could have surely been avoided, because it is impossible to properly examine a terrified, wailing child.

Don't Punish or Ridicule a Child for Being Afraid: There is no point in shouting at or punishing a terrified child. This will only increase his/her fears. Ridiculing a child by calling him/her: coward, crybaby, chicken-hearted, lily-livered, is counter productive. Look at a child's fear from his/her point of view, not an adult one.

A ghost may appear quite real to the child. Making fun and saying that it doesn't exist will not help in anyway. Instead tell him/her: "lots of children your age are afraid of ghosts. It's all right to feel that way." At the same time try to find out what has caused the child to believe in ghosts and plan practical solutions. All children feel more secure when a rational explanation is offered for their fears, even when they do not fully understand it.

The Balancing Act: "Ignore a child's fears at your own peril; be too solicitous and share your bed." Some children feign being afraid in order to manipulate their parents into letting them sleep in the same bed, to extract more attention or to avoid going to school. Parents have to strike a balance between being too concerned and not bothering at all. Both excessive concern and neglect can reinforce a child's fears. If children are rewarded for not being afraid they will soon overcome their fears—pretended or real.

Teasing out Terror: Children must feel safe at all times. If they appear distressed, talk to them about their fears. Talking about fears gives children the opportunity to work out their fears without any sense of shame. Reassure them that fear will diminish and eventually disappear. Stress due to any cause can precipitate or accentuate fears. Shifting of family, change of school, death in the family all can make a child extremely anxious. If parents are understanding and supportive they can reduce the child's anxiety about new adjustments and minimise his/her fears.

When to Seek Professional Help

1. If your child's fears are inappropriate for his or her age.
2. If they have persisted for a long time.
3. If your child regresses to previously outgrown fears.

4. If the child is so terrified that he/she refuses to go to school, is unable to sleep or doesn't let the parent out of sight.

Case Studies

Abhilasha, thirteen, was mortally afraid of cockroaches. The mere sight of these brown creatures was enough to send her into frenzy. When she was a young child she was repeatedly threatened that if she didn't drink milk, eat food or complete her homework, cockroaches would climb on her bed and bite her. Slowly, instead of crevices, the cockroaches started living inside her mind.

To remove her fear, she was shown that just two puffs of an insecticide were enough to kill the cockroaches. She saw for herself that when a cockroach was touched by a stick, it quickly ran away. It took some time but ultimately Abhilasha was able to understand that cockroaches, like all other insects, were after all tiny little things and a big, strong girl like her had no reason to be afraid of them.

Pintoo, seven, was afraid of dogs and started crying the moment he saw a dog come nearby. He had once been bitten by a stray dog and had to take anti-rabies injections. His elder brother Mintoo revelled in terrorising Pintoo with horrifying tales of dangerous dogs.

To remove the fear of dogs (or any other animal) it is necessary that an environment be built which shows the dog to be a friendly and faithful animal. Here is how Pintoo's parents helped him overcome his fear of dogs:

- Mintoo was severely reprimanded and strictly forbidden from frightening Pintoo.
- A framed poster was put up in the children's room showing a young child reclining comfortable against a dog and sipping water from his sipper.
- Pintoo was given a soft toy dog to play with.
- A storybook about a friendly, faithful, brave dog was presented and read out to him.
- Pintoo was taken to the nearby park quite often to let him see other children playing with their pets.

Devyani, nine, was scared of dark. The shadows of a nearby tree cast on her bedroom, the fluttering of curtains in gentle breeze, all combined to create a horrifying illusion. She would remain awake and keep her bedroom lights on, or plead with her parents to let her sleep in their bedroom.

Her parents couldn't accept her fear: "There is nothing to be afraid of, go back to sleep", was their usual, irritated response. They should have realised that the shadows were there and fluttering of curtains was real. This could be quite scary, especially for a little child.

The Right Approach

1. Accept the child's fears as genuine and give reassurance. When you acknowledge that the shadows look scary, the child is more likely to believe in your reassurance that they are harmless.
2. To make the child feel safe you can close the windows and draw curtains. So, neither will the curtains flutter nor will the shadows form.

3. Sit in the child's bed and hold hands till he/she dozes off. After a few days the child will gain confidence and all you would need to do is to tuck him/her up and leave the room.
4. A night lamp helps most children.
5. Leave the interconnecting door ajar.
6. The child may feel happy and relaxed with familiar toys and dolls sharing his/her bed.

Children will have fears, as parents it is your job to help them overcome their fright. You must teach them that there is nothing wrong in being scared or feeling nervous, and that it is possible to master fears.

11

Every Child is Unique

Children develop most satisfactorily if they are loved for what they are, not for what anyone thinks they ought to be.

Anthony Storr

In this world no two human beings are exactly alike, even identical twins behave differently inspite of apparently the same genetic endowment. Every child in some respects is like all other children, but in some he/she is like no other. All children will have many common characteristics, but also some unique traits. Understanding and respecting the uniqueness of each child is the key to successful parenting.

Some children are highly organised, meticulous and confident, while others are extremely disorganised, careless and timid. The first group is able to cope with the stress of examinations, public performances etc. with consummate ease. The other group is unable to face even minor stresses. Thus, during an examination they may become so tense that they make a mess of even those questions to which they know the answers by heart.

This second group needs careful handling and emotional backing. A comprehensive support system should be developed and deployed for them in such a manner that they do not feel helpless and are able to face various challenges with a positive frame of mind.

If parents keep the concept of uniqueness in mind, many problems arising out of unwarranted and unjustified comparisons among children can be avoided. Undue comparisons have the potential to damage a child's personality—seriously and permanently. Without even realising it, parents can make a child feel inferior and unwanted by praising his/her siblings or peers. This is especially damaging if it is done in the background of constant criticism of the child.

Parents cite the example of children who are good in studies or successful in sports, in the fond hope that their children will also be motivated to perform better. If this is done judiciously and skillfully it might help the child, but insensitivity on the part of parents can injure the child's pride and give him/her an inferiority complex. As a consequence, instead of improving, the performance of the child deteriorates.

Why do some children fail inspite of having the potential and favourable conditions, while others surmount all adversities to succeed? It is apparent that the strengths and protective factors in their physical, temperamental and psychological make-up drive these children to attain success. These children seem to be remarkably resilient and are able to triumph over adverse circumstances in ways which can surprise us. Charlie Chaplain was abandoned by his mother and placed in an orphanage when he was a little child. He overcame the emotional trauma to become a successful actor. It seems he turned his own self-esteem problems to advantage by playing 'the tramp.'

Children have different needs. Parents face an eternal dilemma at the dining table because usually what one child likes the other hates. Ladies finger is probably the only vegetable uniformly liked by all children. My elder daughter likes them split longitudinally while the younger one must have small chopped pieces. If both your children are equally doughty and evenly matched in spirit and physique, you will have a harrowing time deciding the menu. But then it was your very own decision to have two children!

It is now well established that **a sense of uniqueness builds self-esteem.** Parents must understand that uniqueness and high self-esteem are interconnected as well as interdependent. If they can make a child feel unique and special, they have scored a major victory.

To develop a sense of uniqueness children need to know there is something special about them and that others also think them special. They need to know and do things that no one else can do. If children are given opportunities to use their imagination and creativity and are allowed to express themselves in their own way they will grow in self-esteem. Children who feel good about their personal characteristics gain confidence and approach things more positively. These children start making efforts to improve their lot and also succeed at receiving approval and respect from others for their achievements.

When a child starts appreciating his/her capabilities and learns to enjoy being different, he/she is destined for success.

Seven Steps to build Your Child's Sense of Uniqueness

Accept Your Child

Accepting the child—all of him/her—including the good and the bad is the first step towards acknowledging that every child is unique. While parents may focus on changing undesirable behaviour, they should not insist upon changing everything about the child to fit their specifications.

It is important that you communicate acceptance of your children by appreciating their assets and praising their accomplishments. You must provide children opportunities to explain their feelings, attitudes, opinions and actions. This can clear many doubts and misunderstandings between parents and children. Remember acceptance of uniqueness is the key to self-esteem.

Point out the Potential

Parents should train themselves to recognise their children's unique abilities and talents. They must point out to children things about them that are different or special. If you find that your daughter sings well, tell her about her gift and try to nurture her talent. Similarly, children may be gifted at chess, computers, mathematics, tennis or cricket. They can develop their unique talents into extremely profitable careers provided they receive proper guidance and necessary assistanace from their parents.

Let Children do things their own Way

Most parents when they see their child writing with the left hand force him/her into using the right hand. Wrong beliefs and taboos are responsible for this practice. By inducing a natural left-hander into becoming a right hander, parents only end up confusing the child and his/her brain.

Each child has a different way of doing things. **Namrata**, eleven, always preferred to take medicines in the form of tablets. Even when she was a three-year old kid she would easily swallow down pills of various sizes. Her elder sister, **Aparajita**, thirteen, till date chokes at the sight of any tablet. She must have medicines as syrups, which have to be given in large quantities because she weighs more than forty kilograms.

The message is clear—**Don't tamper with the child's basic temperament.** Personality traits need modification only if they are likely to harm the child's future prospects.

Allow Children to Express themselves Creatively

Due to a variety of reasons, some children have a poor

sense of their uniqueness. They often declare that they are not good at anything or that they can't achieve any success. Parents should not take these statements lightly as they denote that the child is facing serious problems with his/her self-esteem. Before these feelings blow up into inferiority complex they should try to identify areas in which the child has a special interest. If the child can paint, arrange flowers, sing or play an instrument—he/she should be motivated to take these as hobbies. At the same time parents should bolster the child's sense of uniqueness by praising his/her work.

Treat each Child as an Individual

There are umpteen number of parents whose two kids are exactly opposite in all respects. Obviously, they have inherited the same set of genes, which interact with the same environmental set up. Then why this difference? It has been postulated that even subtle differences in gene patterns can cause major behavioural differences.

Keeping this fact in mind parents should prepare themselves to find apples and oranges growing on the same tree. If parents treat apples as apples and enjoy oranges for being oranges, they will harvest a successful crop.

Facilitate your Child's Learning Style

Some children put on music when they are studying; others want pin drop silence. Some get up early in the morning, while others study late into the night. Parents must identify and support the child's style of learning, provided it is producing the desired results. Trying to alter a child's way of learning may adversely affect his/her academic performance.

I have seen parents asking/forcing the child to read quietly, while he/she prefers to read aloud and can remember the facts better by this method. Parents should understand that these children need both visual and auditory inputs to memorise things.

Loving each Child Best

"Since he was about three, everything to do with Yash has been a struggle", recalls Mrs. Grover. "The first word he ever spoke was 'No', and he is still stuck with it. Before a gift is even given, he is negotiating the next one. When it's study time he throws a tantrum, when it's dinner-time he suddenly loses his appetite and when it's party time he fails to find a single good dress. He seems to take pride in his capacity to send me into a fit."

She further adds, "Yash never lets any chance go a-begging. If his younger brother, Rishi, got a bigger piece of chocolate—he would go to the extent of measuring it with a scale. His teachers are always nicer to his classmates than to him. He is on a constant vigil for any injustice, no matter how slight or unintentional. Rishi on the other hand, is as easy to care for as Yash is difficult. He is organised, self sufficient, responsible and helpful. Unlike Yash he doesn't need constant reminders for—bathing, having breakfast, completing home work etc."

Mrs. Grover Says, "I sometimes think, do I love Rishi more? I blame myself for not being a better mother, more appreciative of and responsive to the needs of Yash. How many times have I promised myself, I will never yell at Yash again; I'll try to remain calm! Moments later I am hollering at him using my lungs to the fullest."

Many parents face a similar predicament, but there is no need to feel guilty or miserable. You love your children with passion, each for very different reasons. If you have one easy-going child, feel happy for the little mercies God bestows on lucky parents. The other more difficult one has been sent to you lest you develop a misguided belief: "Parenting isn't so hard after all."

12

Do you Shout too Much?

Almost all parents admit to shouting at their children but no one thinks it actually works.

P.K.

Shouting at your children to obey is like using a horn to move buffaloes off the road—it produces the same result. Shouting at one's children may contravene all good parenting slogans, but rest assured every parent does it, and agrees that it doesn't work. Family life is such a cauldron of emotions that you have to be a saint to eschew the urge to shout. But then saints don't marry, rear children and raise families.

Is shouting at one's children the ultimate parental taboo? Should parents be censored unequivocally for shouting at their wards? Many people don't seem to think so.

"When angry, count four; when very angry swear" said Mark Twain. And almost all shouters apparently agree that a good yell can clear the air and be liberating and rejuvenating. They sincerely believe that children have to be yelled at to make them tough. Their argument is: "we don't want our children to be fragile flowers who will wilt the moment heat is turned on."

You shout at your kids not because you think it is the best option, but because you feel drained, dominated, exploited, criticised and even humiliated. The stress and strain of modern living takes a heavy toll, and parents are perpetually on the verge of blowing their fuse. A final act of indiscretion on the part of the child brings about an untimely explosion.

No one would advocate shouting as desirable parental behaviour, but it must be remembered that parenting is not a popularity contest which has to be won at any cost. Parents have to instil values, teach proper behaviour and educate their children. This is not an easy task and at times their patience will be tested to its limits. If you're driven up the wall—shout, but do think, whether you could have managed the situation without exercising your lungs too much. The trick is to shout effectively and judiciously.

Shouting at children when they are out of control indirectly means that you have also lost control over your emotions. While an occasional outburst is acceptable, shouting without remission, especially if the parent-child relationship lacks in mutual love, can be devastating for the child's personality.

According to a recent study by psychiatrists at a

hospital affiliated to Harvard Medical School, shouting at children can significantly and permanently alter the structure of their brains. These findings are scary if not downright terrifying, but further research is required to substantiate these early findings.

Before you start worrying that shouting at your children will damage their brains and prior to your getting their brains scanned, let me give you good news! Most children quickly become desensitised to excessive parental ranting and simply switch off. Children of loud parents develop a technique of "downing their shutters" or "switching off their receiving sets" the moment their parental radio station starts its daily broadcast. So, is it the parents who suffer more from their shouting than their children?

One permanent damage relentless shouting can do is that these children become pretty adept shouters themselves and develop volatile personalities. The age of the child is also very important in this context. A young child doesn't understand the difference between shouting and hating and may take parental outbursts as indicating hate and dislike for him/her. With a teenager it is different as he/she is in a better position to reason that your shouting is merely a manifestation of your temporary anguish and in reality you love him/her a lot.

Mrs. Neeta Mehra, a working mother says: "I shout the most at the end of a day, when I am tired or when I have an unusually long list of things to squeeze into an already crowded schedule. I also roar when my children encroach upon the last vestiges of my personal time and space." The triggers are many and varied but stress and exhaustion come high on the list. Maybe low blood sugar levels have something to do with the high incidence of shouting.

Shouting provokes a conflict in the minds of most parents. The turmoil of loving and hating the child at the same time becomes difficult for them to handle. When the realities and disappointments of parenting shatter the dreams of becoming an ideal parent—anxiety and guilt are the net result.

The dilemma, whether to shout or not, has no simple solution. Parents feel guilty if they shout and frustrated when they suppress the urge. Some shouters put themselves on a par with convicted criminals, which in my opinion is an extreme example of self-flagellation.

Five steps to rest your vocal cords

1. Evolve a suitable disciplinary model for your family and stick to it.
2. If your child is upset, angry or frustrated, avoid getting caught in his/her foul mood. Refrain from picking up an unnecessary argument, as it is likely to lead to an entirely avoidable shouting match.
3. Think for a while—are you overdoing it. If yes there is no harm in shutting up and making truce with your child.
4. Evening meals can be used to facilitate communication between the warring parties. Beware! Better communication is not synonymous with 'sermonising.' Avoid lecturing the child at the dining table; instead listen to his/her point of view.

5. If shouting is inevitable, it is better to keep things simple and to speak honestly and without being melodramatic. If you tell the child: "you have made me very angry", it will have a more positive impact than calling him/her a horrible brat or an idiot.

Better Discipline—Lesser Shouting

The Oxford Dictionary of Current English describes 'Discipline' as—1. Training or way of life aimed at self-control and conformity. 2. A control or order exercised over people or animals.

Any animal trainer will tell you that training animals is relatively easy because you can starve them or use a cane. Dealing with children is a different proposition altogether. You can't starve and you shouldn't use caning as a disciplining technique. When you try to discipline your child, you are dealing with an extremely versatile and sensitive brain, capable of reasoning and decision making. So the onus is on you to be equally reasonable, imaginative and compassionate.

Regarding discipline most parents are confused as to what constitutes a too strict or too lenient attitude. Too strict an approach is likely to head to confrontation. Too lenient an attitude is commensurate with disobedience, disregard and even delinquency. The three cardinal rules for effective disciplining are:

- Be realistic
- Be consistent
- Be supportive

Moving Towards Better Discipline

1. Have guidelines and implement them consistently:

Having a set of guidelines for proper behaviour is the first step in the direction of controlling impropriety. If children are bound by well-defined limits, the chances are they will remain within them. Laxity in implementing the set rules is likely to result in unnecessary tension and frequent inappropriate behaviour. It is important that appropriate behaviour is rewarded and negative behaviour punished, but more important is the consistency of such rewards and punishments. Consistency of discipline helps the child in developing a frame of reference, which leads to a fair degree of uniformity in his/her behaviour pattern.

2. Reward and Punishment

Reward. Who doesn't want recognition for good work or deed? Children specially need a pat on the back for conforming to the prescribed norms of behaviour. Punishment only acts as a deterrent, it tells the child what not to do, but rewards teach the accepted and expected behaviour. They also reinforce such behaviour and are a must if long-term changes are desired.

Parents may feel that there is no need to reward a child for doing what is expected. But they must realise that children have only a vague concept of what is expected and what isn't. In doing what is expected, the child is making a special effort and this must be appreciated. Rewarding your child for brushing at night without being told to do so, reinforces the continuation of the habit. Rewards can be in any of the following forms:

- Monetary
- Verbal praise
- Written notes of thanks
- Extra time to play or watch TV
- A small gift
- Delayed bed time
- A spontaneous hug

Punishment: Choosing appropriate punishment for inappropriate behaviour is definitely more difficult than giving rewards. Parents should avoid harsh and impracticable punishments e.g.—"no picnics or eating out till you improve your ranks." This may dishearten the child and can cause rebellion. Even worse, you will have to sit at home on weekends, do the cooking and feed your convict.

Asking the child to stand in a corner for ten minutes can be controlled but making him/her stand for full sixty minutes may be difficult to implement. Some urgent work may require your immediate attention and the child will simply vanish from the scene. Leaving a punishment incomplete will not have the desired effect; on the contrary it can make the child more obstinate and difficult to manage.

Never trade a punishment for a reward on the D.S.E. (Disciplinary Stock Exchange). Punishment for a misdeed should not be nullified by a reward for good behaviour; both must be dealt with separately. What do you do if your child completes his/her homework but leaves the study table in a mess? Praise the child for finishing his/her assignment, but at the same time reprimand him/her for not cleaning the table. It would be wrong to say: "OK as you have done your homework, it more than makes up for leaving your table in a mess." If you begin trading in discipline, your child is bound to learn the trade quickly. He/she will prove to be an astute businessman picking up bargain deals, but getting undisciplined in the bargain.

3. U.P.F.—The United Parent Front:

While disciplining a child parents must put up a united front. If one parent disagrees with the other's tactics, it should be discussed at a private moment. Open disagreement regarding a disciplinary action not only confuses the child but makes him/her bitter towards the seemingly unjust parent. As described earlier, if you have clear guidelines for acceptable/unacceptable behaviour, this situation need not arise.

Never ever shift the responsibility of disciplining on your spouse. "Wait until your father comes home"—is a common refrain of many mothers. This must be avoided at all costs as it gives a negative message to the child. It implies that you are incapable of controlling the situation, and can make the child more belligerent. By relinquishing disciplinary powers to your husband you place him in an unenviable situation. His personality acquires fearsome proportions for the child.

Disciplining is a physically and mentally draining job. Even before you finish patting yourself for successfully managing a tricky situation, a fresh crisis arises. You can run out of ideas and techniques to deal with the indiscipline of your child and your frustration levels may rise. In these circumstances, delay dealing with children immediately. Send them to their room and tell them that you will deal with this later. Delaying allows you to regain your control and recoup your energy. Delay also reduces impractical consequences as it allows for a different perspective than that viewed at the height of anger.

Sometimes one parent chooses to hide the child's indiscipline from another parent. This may be justified when it is done to protect the child from a parent who is known to be violent and abusive. Such protection can salvage the child's personality from total devastation. However, concealing children's inappropriate behaviour actually increases their anxiety level and they get the message that the other parent should be feared. They start fantasising about the fatal consequences should the stricter parent find out their inappropriate behaviour. In most cases it is better for the child to face the music from both speakers—one producing bass and the other treble.

4. Taming the Tempest

If a child is upset or angry and speaks out his/her mind without being abusive or destructive let him/her do so. Vocalisation of frustration and anger reduces the child's tension and must be tolerated by parents. However screaming and cursing should not be permitted, especially if it is directed at the parents. Limits must be set and the child should be taught appropriate ways of venting his/her feelings. Allowing the child to get away with verbal abuse can be very damaging in the long run.

Temper Tantrums: Tackling temper tantrums requires a lot of patience, some firmness and a little bit of foresight. Children have a knack of choosing the most inopportune place and time for throwing a tantrum, such as: a relative's place, a crowded market, an ice-cream parlour and so on. Be patient and let the child calm down if the scene is being enacted at home. You have to be firm and in control if it occurs at a relative's or a friend's place. Finally, you must have the foresight to avoid toyshops and ice cream parlours as far as possible when you go the market with your child.

'Don'ts' to deal with Temper Tantrums

- Don't allow the child to have an audience for displaying his/her histrionics. Remove him/her to a room or any other isolated area.
- Don't try to reason with your child when he/she is in this state.
- Don't hesitate to tell the child that there will be a consequence later for his/her bad behaviour.
- Don't delay rewarding a child who check or aborts a tantrum spontaneously to communicate with you.

For many parents the use of discipline and reward remains a perplexing problem. Lack of consistency in dealing with inappropriate behaviour further complicates matters. Having a set of guidelines and implementing them with consistency can prevent the situation from getting out of hand. The discipline chart is an important tool, with positive and negative consequences, which can simplify the difficult but rewarding job of child rearing.

Weekly Discipline Chart

Name   Grand Total   Grading

S. No.	Rule	Mon	Tue	Wed	Thu	Fri	Sat
1	Getting up on time						
2	Brushing teeth in the morning						
3	Punctuality at school						
4	Completing the assignments						
5	Keeping the room clean						
6	Taking proper diet						
7	Reading newspaper (Headlines atleast)						
8	Not using the telephone unnecessarily						
9	Watching TV as permitted						
10	Helping in household chores						
11	Not cursing						
12	Participating in outdoor activity/games						
13	Avoiding chocolates at night						
14	Brushing teeth at night						
15	Going to bed on the agreed hour						
	Total						

- You can substitute the items as per your special needs.
- Give 1 or 0 for compliance or non-compliance of each item.
- Maximum achievable score is 90.
- Reward/consequence should be distributed as per the grade attained.
- Grading. Above 75 — Good
  Between 50-75 — Fair
  Below 50 — Poor

13

Good Parents Communicate Better

The ability to communicate effectively has made humans the most successful race on earth.

P.K.

Communication with children has two distinct aspects to it—quantity and quality. Both are important for the development of a balanced personality. Lack of communication or faulty communication both can adversely affect the child's psyche.

Lack of communication. Children grow up so fast that parents who lose the opportunity of communicating with their children when they were young, may never develop meaningful and warm relationship with them in later life. Lack of communication between parents and children is the bane of modern society. The more successful the parents, the more preoccupied they are—with their careers and with their social engagements. Naturally, inspite of their sincere efforts they are unable to find sufficient time for the their children.

Television is an important factor in decreasing communication within the family. Most middle class families spend their entire evening watching never ending serials while children remain glued to the screen waiting eagerly for the so called 'short breaks' when the advertisements are aired.

Communication-deprived children suffer from delayed speech development and demonstrate poor social adjustments. Their academic performance is also below par. The more you talk and interact with your child the faster his/her brain matures. Children who have prolonged, frequent contacts with their parents have been known to demonstrate a higher IQ, they are also more stable emotionally and more successful socially.

Faulty Communication. This is perhaps even more damaging to the child's psychosocial development than mere lack of communication. Parents can alienate their children by their thoughtless words thereby closing all channels for future communication. Unfortunately many parents do not realise the importance of proper communication with their children. Their communication sessions with children generally end up as sermons or arguments. The worst offenders are parents whose interaction with their children are inadequate as well as inappropriate.

Ten Tips for Better Communication

Good communication skills are the basis of any successful relationship, whether between husband and wife or parents and children. Many parents face problems while communicating with their children. I hope the following tips will help parents to communicate better with their children.

1. Talking + Listening = Communication

The basic mistake that parents make is, they talk but never listen. While communicating, the flow of ideas and thoughts should necessarily be bi-directional otherwise it becomes a lecture. The child must know that when you finish talking, he/she will get a chance to speak. Try listening actively. Make encouraging gestures and sounds—nod your head, say yes, right, that's fine.

Avoid: "You listen to me."
Try: "I want you to listen to me and then you can speak and I'll listen."

2. Don't Begin With Accusation

If you start the conversation with an accusation, the child will end it with a brief refusal. If your opening line is: "Why did you break the wall clock?" The most likely answer you'll get is: "I didn't."

The better approach would be to ask: "How did the clock break?" This will get the conversation going and you will receive a detailed account of the events leading to the breaking of clock. You can also utilise this opportunity to teach the child to be more responsible in future.

Avoid: "I don't believe you."
Try: "Promise not to lie and I'll believe you."

3. Avoid Flowery language

Reserve your eloquence for boardroom meetings, farewell parties and the like. While communicating with children it is better to keep things straight and simple. It is especially important when dealing with a relatively young child because more often than not, the child will either miss the point or misinterpret it. In case of older children use of flowery language can injure their pride and give them an inferiority complex.

Avoid: "You are an idiot of the highest order."
Try: "You need to apply yourself more."
Avoid: "Your room is worse than a pigsty."
Try: "Your room needs urgent cleaning."

4. Words are Like Bullets

There is no denying the power of spoken words; they are more potent than bullets. You can use them to attack or protect your child's personality. If children feel they are being attacked they may:

- Clam up
- Start arguing
- Throw counter accusations

All the three situations interrupt the flow of

communication, and may alienate the child. As a rule communication will deteriorate if you use abusive languages. Parents who try to browbeat their child all the time, may succeed initially but gradually the child will start paying back in the same coin. While dealing with children a mild attitude and milder vocabulary usually produces the desired result.

Avoid: "Come here immediately."
Try: "Let's get together in five minutes."
Avoid: "I want you home by six positively."
Try: "Please be home between six and six thirty."

5. Prevent Misinterpretation

Remember children are not expert face readers, so they cannot decipher the real reason behind your grim expression. In most instances they will misread the look on a parent's face and presume that they have done something wrong.

If parents are upset or angry because of a job-related problem or there is some other reason, they must let their children know about it in a verbal way. There is no need to go into details, just tell the child: "Something/someone has made me very angry, but it has nothing to do with you. Let me have tea and rest for a while then I'll feel much better".

This small, thoughtful piece of communication will not only relieve the child's anxiety, it can make him/her more favourably inclined towards you.

6. Written Notes are Great

There are occasions when you need to communicate your feelings in writing. Parents and children should use this method more often as written communication gives an opportunity to phrase thoughts more coherently. Notes praising children for good behaviour, helping in housework or doing well in studies are great morale boosters. Parents can pleasantly surprise their children by slipping a message in their pencil box or note book saying that they love them very much, or they are proud of them.

Notes can also be used to register a complaint without creating a scene. When you expect a showdown or want to avoid an unnecessary argument, written notes are the best way to show your displeasure.

7. Wordless Communication

An important means of communicating with children is through eye contact and change of facial expression. When you are socialising or in a setting where it is not possible to give verbal commands you can show your approval or disapproval by an encouraging or a stern look. Success of this form of communication depends upon prior conditioning of the child. Inspite of your best training, sometimes the child may avoid your eyes to act according to his/her wishes. Don't get upset, children after all are children.

8. Demonstrative Communication

All human beings are born with a need to be loved and never outgrow it. When it comes to communicating feelings of love and caring, many parents are found wanting. Many of us got our first real proof of parental love when we fell sick. This seems to imply that illness, injury and other adverse situations are a prerequisite for receiving love and care. Parents must take care that children do not get such distorted picture of parent-child relations. The line: "If you love somebody, show it", may sound cliched but it nevertheless works wonders. So try to demonstrate your love, show you care and express your feelings.

Demonstrative communication can be 'verbal' or 'physical'. Some verbal statements you can use are:

- "I am really proud to have a son/daughter like you."
- "If I scold you it doesn't mean that I don't love you."
- "I am lucky to have such a conscientious/dependable/meticulous child like you."

Don't assume your child knows that you feel this way, communicate to him/her in your own words.

Physical demonstration of feelings is also very important for the development of a warm and loving parent-child relationship. Never miss an opportunity to hug, kiss, or cuddle your child. If you don't give love today, your child will not learn to receive it tomorrow—neither from you nor from anyone else. It has been observed that such children are non-demonstrative themselves and may have unproductive relationships in later life. Children who have plenty of emotional and physical contact with their parents find it easier to give and receive love.

9. Supportive Communication

For proper expression of emotion and to sustain communication a good vocabulary is a must. Children may face problems while communicating because they lack experience in labeling their feelings. When children fail to find appropriate words and are unable to correctly verbalise their internal feelings they are likely to become frustrated. Frustration may cause behavioural problems and destructive tendencies. Sometimes in their haste they may choose the wrong words and offend their parents. Thus the process of communication may deteriorate into an argument.

Parents must help their children to correctly label a feeling or emotion. Here are some examples, which can be used to assist the child:

- "I get the feeling from your behaviour that you are trying to say ———"
- "While you sound angry, it is actually your frustration over ———"
- "I guess you want to communicate that ———"

10. Anticipatory Communication

A good parent can anticipate the child's mood and reaction to a situation. If you are observant enough you can see some-non-verbal reaction: a dull look, a deadpan face, brimming eyes or intense denial. If you can latch on to these expressions you will have instant access to the child's emotional turmoil. The child will also have an easier time communicating with you because he/she can sense your involvement and concern. Parents who are good at anticipatory communication have a very good chance of identifying and dealing with the child's problems.

14

A Born Leader?

Real leaders are ordinary people with extraordinary determination.

Hughes M.

There is a general belief that leadership is an in-built quality. We seem to think that some people are born to lead, while rest are destined to follow. Genes do count in determining performance, but they can't account for every achievement. There are innumerable examples where apparently ordinary individuals have risen to great heights and led people, communities and nations to glory.

Leaders are not born—they are made. Children who become head boys/girls, young men and women who captain sports teams, senior executives who run organisations are all products of conscientious parents who worked hard on fostering leadership qualities in their wards.

What is leadership mentality?

1. Ability to think independently.
2. Mental strength to tackle tough situations.
3. Positive attitude to prevail over adversities.
4. Capacity to plan strategy.
5. Sound moral character—just and truthful.
6. Readiness to share.
7. Initiative to start new ventures.
8. The ability to feel good about one self and make others happy.
9. Natural curiosity and enthusiasm towards life.

The Leadership Equation:

$$R\ 3 + D\ 3 = \text{Leader}$$

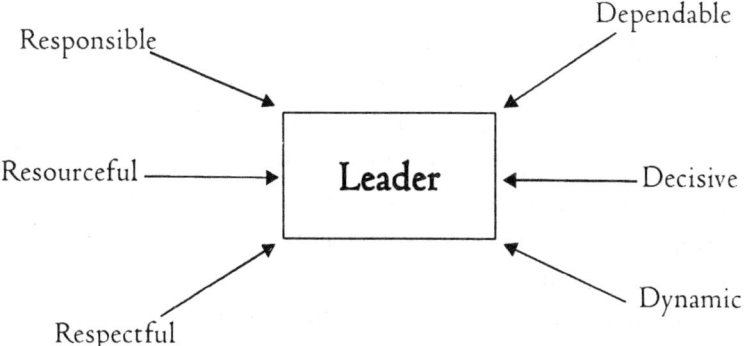

You too can make your child a Leader

All children are born with the same number of chromosomes, they have an identical brain structure and similar body functions. The edge comes from mental attitude, character and strategy. It is in these vital areas that parents have to help their children so that not only do they achieve their potential but exceed it. Success and self-belief join hands to make a leader out of an ordinary person. Let me share some secrets on how to develop a leadership mentality.

1. *Begin Early.* A leadership mentality will benefit the child at all stages of his/her life. It has been observed that leadership during school years and achievements in extracurricular activities are more accurate predictors of adult success than IQ or examination percentage. Nurturing self-esteem is crucial in inspiring a child to peak performance, and you can't start too early because once the feelings of incompetence/inadequacy take root, they are very difficult to remove.

2. *What you put in is what you get back.* We all know that if we provide a nutritious diet we will get a healthy child. This applies to character development also. Instilling proper values will make a child grow in inner strength. The associated confidence will transform him/her into a leader.

3. *Assess your child's Potential.* Wrong assessment of the child's potential and an attempt to mould him/her contrary to his/her natural ability can lead to disaster. Although listening to the child's views is recommended,

his/her self-assessment may suffer from inexperience. There is no harm in taking expert, outside help in shaping your child's future.

According to a newspaper report, Sachin Tendulkar—the modern cricketing legend—had gone to Dennis Lillee—the great Australian fast baller—to learn the art of pace bowling. Lillee was not impressed by the young boy—at all. Few years later Lillee saw Tendulkar bat and this time he was highly impressed by the young man's brilliant shots. Sachin's coach Ramakant Achrekar had turned him into an explosive, high-class batsman. Today Sachin is an inspiration for every budding Indian cricketer and is regarded as the best batsman in the world.

4. *Focus on Inappropriate Behaviour not the Personality.* Unfortunately, most parents instead of pointing out the unacceptable behaviour point a finger at the child. "You are so dumb!" "Why can't you get it through your thick skull?" "God, you are such a clumsy, insufferable fool." Criticise the behaviour, not the child. After telling "that's wrong!" explain what's right. You must let your children know what you want them to do, not just what you don't want them to do.

Remember your child is not stupid! If he/she fails to measure up to your yardsticks of excellence—lower them or put in a concerted effort to raise the child's standard. Children who grow up in homes where personalities are attacked tend to develop an inferiority complex.

When confronting the child's act try using phrases like, "poor judgement," "this is not how it is done," "your behaviour was inappropriate." Focusing on the act allows children to save face. It may also allow them to understand better and accept more appropriate options for the next time. This will certainly improve their popularity, especially among their peers. Gaining acceptance in the peer group gives children opportunities to interact, influence and lead other children.

5. *Don't be a Miser with Praise.* Praise is the best tonic for self-esteem; applause the greatest booster of self-confidence. When your little one takes the first few unsteady steps towards you or when he/she climbs up the stairs and declares triumphantly from the top—"I am the tallest"—your look of genuine pleasure and approval makes him/her grow in self-esteem.

A hesitant child may accomplish the feat if he/she is told, "I know you can do it!" And if the parents follow it up with "You did a terrific job", the child's confidence gets a permanent boost.

So many world class sportspersons, singers, musicians and academicians readily concede that the primary influence on their early career was their parent's support and appreciation. Talking positively about children and their accomplishments reinforces self-image and goads them to strive for further excellence. It is through exemplary performance that one finally gains leadership.

Any success however small, is worth complimenting but don't go overboard with your praise. Constructive criticism coupled with sincere wholehearted appreciation is the winning formula. Insincere and exaggerated praise may inflate the child's ego unnecessarily and is a sure recipe for failure.

6. Think about Success not Obstacles.

> "What if I fail?" (The test)
> "What if I forget?" (The speech)
> "What if I miss?" (The goal)

Individuals who instead of focusing on how to succeed, keep worrying about how to avoid failure generally end up as disappointments. Parents should try to develop right values and a positive attitude in their wards. They should persuade them to concentrate on success and to be pragmatic about failures and treat them as temporary setbacks. The person who believes in success is the one who inspires others to follow.

7. Build on Previous Accomplishments. If your child has won a medal in a debate competition, a cup in athletics or a certificate of merit in academics-keep it displayed prominently in the house. Whenever the child sees it he/she will get an urge to do better. Confining to previous triumphs is not good but using them as inspiration for additional success is recommended. By seeing the previously won medals and trophies the child gets the message: "I have done it in the past, I can do it again." This 'can do' approach can make your child a leader.

8. Teach your Child to Relax. Ability to remain calm in a crisis identifies the ace in the pack. Teach your child to relax because anxiety leads to poor concentration, which is the root cause of poor performance. A relaxed mind can think and act better, thus improving the efficiency of a person.

An extremely effective technique to relax is to breathe deeply and evenly. Train the child to concentrate on each inspiration and expiration and to let his/her mind go blank for a few moments. Thinking of a favourite song, imagining a flowing river or a cool breeze blowing gently—any pleasant idea can be utilised to put the child in a relaxed mood.

9. *Let Children Experiment.* We admire and follow someone who is willing to experiment, to rise to challenges. Yet when it comes to our own children we want them to play safe. All too often we step in and try to shield a child from mistakes. In the process we deprive him/her of the important learning experiences.

Parents should motivate the child to take initiative and to tackle new challenges. One who tries, fails, rectifies his/her mistakes and gets up to make a fresh attempt finally succeeds. This spirit of adventure and steely resolve sets the leader apart. A true leader is one who rises to the occasion without fear of failure and is able to inspire others by his/her enthusiasm.

10. *Leaders are Dreamers.* If your son wants to be a fighter jet pilot or your daughter wants to become a crime reporter-what would your response be? "It's risky business! Why can't you think of something less dangerous?"

The chances are your son may go into aerodesigning and your daughter might become a computer programmer. Don't overreact, let children fantasise about the future. Who knows they may devise means and find ways to make their fantasies come true.

To see things you should have vision; to visualise future you must have dreams. Leaders have vision and they can dream. They look at things differently and can explain them to others. They are able to influence people into following their path. So let children dream but tell them that the best way to make their dreams come true is to wake up and work.

11. *Give Children Opportunities to Lead.* Leadership like any other skill has to be learnt, practised and mastered. Just as a tennis player must practise hard to perfect his/her serve, a would-be leader must be provided ample opportunities to imbibe leadership skills.

Motivate the child to become a member of NCC, NSS, Scouts or other such groups, which give a platform to interact with and lead other children. A captain of a school football team, a class monitor or a school prefect—all are learning the craft of leadership. Parents must encourage this early apprenticeship but the child should be allowed to pursue his/her own area of interest. Some children revel on stage, some shine on the playground while still others excel in the classroom. Allowing children to operate in their favoured domain builds their confidence and lays the foundation of leadership.

Some leadership avenues worth exploring:

Editorship of the school magazine.	If the child has a flair for writing.
Membership of school quiz team.	If the child remembers facts easily.
Participation in elocution and debate competitions	If the child has good command over languages.
Involvement in—group discussions.	If the child shows good grasping and expressive powers.

The three Universal "S'—Studies, Sport and Stage remain the most sought after pursuits for most aspiring leaders.

12. *A smile takes you a Mile.* I read somewhere that it requires sixty-four facial muscles to frown and only fourteen to smile. So why overwork your face? A friendly hello and a pleasant smile can win many a battle. Teach your child to not only greet those in his/her own circle but others as well. Instil in him/her human values and respect for elders. A person who exudes natural warmth and genuine compassion is quickly recognised as potential leader.

13. *Your Example Matters.* It has been seen that when parents exhibit leadership qualities, it becomes easier for children to develop similar traits. Parents who set high standards of moral and ethical conduct generally succeed in teaching the same to their children. Like begets like. A thief can't expect his son to be a virtuous, law-abiding citizen. An honest, resourceful father is likely to have a respectful, responsible son.

A shortcut to success has not yet been successfully developed. Making of a leader is a gradual process, which requires parental support, encouragement and hard work. These efforts pay off doubly, firstly in the form of development of leadership qualities in the child and more importantly in the formation of close, warm relationship between the parents and the child.

15

The Horror Called-Homework

Father: What happened to your homework?
Son: I made it into a plane and someone hijacked it.

It's a cold December night-the time is 9 PM. An exasperated Mrs. Jain and her fatigued eleven-year-old daughter **Diksha** are struggling to finish the never-ending homework. They have been at it all evening, they haven't had dinner and the Maths assignment is still not complete. To top it all, there is also some craft-work to be completed and handed over in the morning.

Every night in millions of homes across the country similar scenes are enacted with alarming regularity. The actors may be different but the script usually remains the same. Although the problem of homework is an age-old one the pressure of the present educational system has turned it into a recurring nightmare for most families.

Homework has degenerated into a form of forced labour, in which pages upon pages of work are heaped upon the child. The child is expected to work like a slave and hardly any scope is provided for improvisation, ingenuity or originality.

Diksha's Daily Schedule

6.00 AM	–	Gets up for school
6.45 AM	–	Departs by the school bus
2.30 PM	–	Back home
3.30 PM	–	Leaves for science tuition
5.00 PM	–	Back home
5.30 PM	–	Leaves for Maths tuition
7.00 PM	–	Back home
7.30-9.00PM	–	Home work

Add to it the pressure of:
- Unit tests, terminals, finals.
- Projects.
- Social pressures-Birthday parties, socialising by parents.

There are innumerable children like Diksha who encounter such sustained stress day in and day out. Imagine the plight of a child who doesn't perform well even after such a backbreaking schedule. Think about the parents who work throughout the day and on coming back home sit for hours with their children helping them with their homework. It's not difficult to visualise the frustrations of highly qualified parents who teach nuclear physics and genetics during the day and revert to teaching

'Cow has four legs' in the evening. What is difficult to understand is that why don't they go bonkers!

It must be said to the credit of most parents that they are always prepared to assist and work alongside their children on homework. The approach and methodology may vary. Some parents restrict themselves to brief occasional explanations while others may go the extent of completing the task themselves. Children are primarily responsible for this difference in parental approach. Some children by nature are sincere and hard working and are able to cope without much supervision or help. In contrast many children have studies at the end of their agenda, if at all. They are immune to parental cajoling or reasoning and often threats and bribery also fail to convince them to study. While trying to make these children do their homework parents should take care not to get irritated, angry or disappointed.

Tips to Tackle Home Work Successfully

1. *Fix Schedule.* Homework—loads of it, is given to children on a daily basis. If there is no daily roster for doing homework, it will either remain incomplete or will be done haphazardly at the last moment, creating a lot of tension and anxiety for both-the child and the parent. As far as fixing the time is concerned, give children the liberty to decide it. Some children prefer to do their homework as soon as they return from school, others may choose to do it later in the evening. However, once the time is fixed, it should be adhered to as realistically as possible. Parents must ensure that during this period no

interruptions in the form of phone calls, TV etc are allowed.

Initially parents may have to remind the child to sit down for studies but gradually this will become a habit. Once this happens the daily pleadings, chiding and threats to study may not be required and this may improve the parent-child relationship.

2. *Don't begin with the Toughest Assignment.* If children have four things to do, let them finish the three easy ones first. This makes them feel happy and relaxed because they now have only one assignment left even though it may be a more difficult task. It also boosts their confidence and they are able to tackle the tough assignment with greater assurance. On the contrary if the child starts with a difficult task he/she may either get bogged down or consume the entire time in finishing a single assignment. This may give rise to frustration and feelings of inadequacy.

3. *An Alternate Strategy.* Most teachers and parents recommend reading the chapter prior to solving questions. I think it's a good idea to read the questions before reading the chapter. By using this strategy the child will have an idea of what he/she should be looking for and concentrating on while going though the chapter. Give the child a pencil and suggest that he/she mark the passages, which seem related to the questions given at the end of the chapter. Thus the child will be able to pinpoint relevant, important information in the first reading itself. This will help the child when he/she has to refer back to several pages in the chapter in search of answers.

4. *Facilitate Independent Working.* Parents should try to avoid sitting next to the child while he/she is doing homework. This is easier said than done because most children stop working the moment parents stop giving them undivided attention. It's not that they can't work, they choose not to work. Once the child develops this dependence he/she is unable to function independently in the classroom also and brings unfinished classwork home. After a busy, tiring day, when parents are faced with the prospect of sitting with the child for hours doing homework they are likely to get frustrated and lose their temper.

If you are trapped in the situation where the child refuses to work without your presence and assistance, you should not break away all at once. Try to get the child gradually used to studying alone in your absence. Initially sit at the far end of the room for a few days. Then start moving out of the room for brief periods and gradually increase the period of your absences until the child is working alone.

There is no fixed age when parents should give their children responsibility of their own studies. It is generally through trial-and-error method that parents come to know whether the child is ready to take independent charge. This however does not mean that parents shouldn't keep track of the child's study schedule. In fact suggestions, supervision and support, will always be needed by the child at every stage of his/her academic career.

5. *Zero in on Correct Problems First.* While checking the child's homework, first praise him for the sums solved

correctly or for getting the spellings of difficult words right. Even for the incorrect ones don't use criticism, instead say, "Please check these again, I am sure you will get the correct answers." The child will not feel offended and will redo the exercises with confidence.

Some parents have a habit of zeroing in on the incorrect problems first. This makes them angry and the resulting outburst upsets the child greatly. The child may develop feelings of animosity or helplessness and his/her work, instead of improving may actually deteriorate.

6. *Split the Assignment.* Most children benefit if the assignment is divided into smaller parts and immediate feedback is given. Let your child solve three problems and then come back to you for checking. Give encouragement for the correct ones and send the child back to do the next lot. By providing the child with immediate feedback and approval you motivate him/her to tackle the next task with renewed vigour. Another advantage is that if the child is doing the assignment incorrectly, the error can be detected and explained right at the beginning, saving the child from having to repeat the entire assignment again.

Once the child's homework is checked and ready he/she will have a feeling of accomplishment and a sense of security that the work is correct. This makes the child more confident in the class and his/her academic performance may improve substantially.

7. *One + One = Eleven!* Children retain information better if it is provided through multiple sensory inputs. It has been observed that a combination of auditory and visual inputs is more effective than either alone. Parents

can tape record some especially bothersome chapters so that the child can listen and read simultaneously. They can record a favourite song or joke in between to cheer up the child.

8. *Avoid Theatrics.* Grimaces, sighs, raising of eyebrows, throwing up of hands–some parents behave as if they are enacting a tragic scene rather than helping the child with homework. Negative body language must be avoided because it only adds to the tension of doing homework. If parents allow themselves to become agitated they will make the child anxious and undermine his/her ability to perform satisfactorily.

9. *Avoid doing you Child's Homework.* Some parents don't have the time or patience to sit for hours while the child does the homework. Others may feel the assignment is too difficult for the child to handle. Whatever the reason, when parents finish their child's homework, the end result is always very damaging. The child develops a feeling of inadequacy and failure and may become increasingly dependent upon the parents for academic work.

10. *It's better to end the Agony.* If the child has been working on his/her assignment for quite some time without making any worthwhile progress, it's better to end his/her agony by stopping the homework. What the child has not accomplished in thirty minutes, he/she is not likely to achieve in next three hours thirty minutes also. Making the child sit indefinitely will only strengthen his/her feelings of incompetence and inadequacy. If the child is unable to do his/her homework once in a while you shouldn't get worried, but if this is

a pattern you should start looking for the cause and take remedial measures.

Inability to Cope with Homework

S. No.	Probable Cause	Remedy
1.	The child may not have understood the concept in class and therefore is not able to finish the assignment at home.	Write a note to the teacher explaining the circumstances Your meeting the teacher may help the child.
2.	The child may already have developed feelings of helplessness and dependency and may wait for you to complete the assignment.	Try to facilitate independent working. Work towards building the child's confidence and improving his academic self-concept.
3.	The child may be suffering from learning disability.	Refer to the chapter—The Problem Child.

In our highly competitive society where we compete for almost everything and practically anything, achievement of good academic grades by the child tops the priority list of every parent. The outstanding students get into good institutions and better jobs. This is the dream and motive of all parents. However, it is this desire that can lead to anxiety, tension and failure, if the wrong approach and techniques are adopted right at the beginning of a child's academic career. Parents must try to inculcate regular and independent study habits in their wards. At the same time they should avoid being overzealous otherwise the child may develop a pathological revulsion towards studies.

16

Friends are Important

If you can boast of five houses but don't have five friends to visit them, you really have invested poorly.
P.K.

Life's warmest and most enduring friendships are forged in childhood. Sharing the joys and pains of growing up together creates an unbreakable bond, which provides children with emotional security and a sense of belonging all through their lives.

Mehul Khanna, eight, was standing, all alone at the edge of the playground watching children play cricket. His family had moved in that locality only a few days ago and he was having trouble making new friends. He didn't notice his father coming and standing behind him, but his father noticed his child's loneliness and decided to help him. At the end of the game he took Mehul to his colleague,

Mr. Verma's house, which was in the same area. Mr. Verma's son Udit was about Mehul's age. Both soon started talking about their favourite cricketers and Udit invited Mehul to join his team.

Their friendship grew over the years, weathering many major and minor storms. They went to different colleges and took up jobs in different cities but always managed to keep in touch. Although Mehul married first, Udit beat him to achieve fatherhood first.

When Mehul's father died of stomach cancer, Udit was with him—in the hospital, at the cremation. Two years later tragedy struck Udit—his daughter died of Hepatitis B. Simultaneously he lost heavily on the share market and his company which he had started a few years back was on the verge of being declared bankrupt. Mehul provided him with emotional as well as financial support. "We've been through difficult times together", Mehul reminded him. "And you've always come through a stronger person. God only tests those who have the strength to face any ordeal."

Thanks to his friend's support Udit rebuilt his life and his business. Within a year Udit Verma was again among the top share brokers on the Mumbai Stock Exchange. A friend is someone who is on and by your side in bad times. Life is full of twists and turns—enough to shake your confidence. A friend helps re-establish your faith in yourself.

Friends are a bridge between the family and the outside world. They provide opportunities to practise and perfect myriad skills needed to succeed in various intimate human relationships in later life. Whatever be the family or social environment, friends have an important influence on the child's personality and his approach towards life—his style of working, accomplishments, thoughts, emotions, taboos, clothes, food habits, addictions etc.

All children want to be accepted, respected and supported by their peers. When they fail to develop a harmonious relationship with other children or face rejection they may withdraw into a shell. This loneliness can slowly but surely lead to the development of inferiority complex.

Some children face problems while interacting with peers and are unable to make friends easily. Proper guidance and assistance from parents can help them overcome their inhibitions. Although parents cannot directly control their child's social life, they certainly can help him/her develop right attitudes towards friends and friendships.

How to help your child make friends

1. Act as a Facilitator

Parents must involve themselves with their child's friends- closely but discreetly. Many parents presume that their children will make friends automatically. This is a false notion. Children may get to know each other through casual meetings but true friendships only develop when children get to meet each other regularly.

Parents should take their roles as facilitators seriously and sincerely. If they find that their child is in the process of developing a special bond with one of his/her friends, they should help him/her in any way they can. Dropping the child at or picking him up from the friend's place is one such small contribution they can make.

Arpita's parents overruled her objections and sent her to a summer camp, which provided training in dramatics, swimming, horse riding etc. Arpita met Bhavana at the camp and their mutual interest in dramatics made them friends. The camp became the stage where they developed their acting skills and their friendship. Parents should give children ample opportunities to meet, interact and evolve as friends.

2. Provide Proper Perspective

When a family moves to a new town the child loses his/her friends. The loss of old friends and the struggle to find new ones can cause sadness, irritability and anxiety. The child feels lonely but his/her vanity makes it hard for him/her to talk about it. Parents must devise ways of giving emotional support without hurting the child's dignity.

This happened to **Dhruv** when his father took up a new job in a new city. He became lonely and anxious, but couldn't talk about it—after all he was now a grown up thirteen-year old! Dhruv's mother sensed her son's turmoil and decided to help him. She dug out some old letters and showed them to Dhruv. These she had received from her childhood friends, with some of whom she was still in contact. She told him: "Everybody faces problems like this at one time or another. I also suffered when I lost my close friends, but I managed to keep in touch with them through letters. You too can write to your friends and share your experiences. You must keep the old relationships going while you try to enter into new ones." Things fell into perspective and Dhruv worked on making new friends while maintaining old friendships.

3. Don't Impose Yourself

While involvement with the child and his/her friends is expected and recommended, parents should not impose their will regarding which friends to keep and which to shun. Although children need guidance they must be allowed to take some of their own decisions. Parents should give them enough leeway to experiment and find out for themselves which friendships work and which ones don't.

Similar age group and socio-economic status do play a role. However, children who think alike usually develop a special bond. In most instances all that parents have to do is to resolve the difficult and contentious issues which may threaten the friendship.

It is natural for parents to want their children not to make wrong friends or become part of an undesirable/ delinquent gang. They may have to take harsh decisions if they feel that the child's friends will adversely affect his/ her future. If parents foresee this danger they should put their foot down—firmly but without making much noise. Parents, who succeed in instilling right values and a positive self-image, give the child the necessary confidence to differentiate between good and bad friends.

4. Let children be trendy, if not trend-setters

Parents often censure children for clothes, hairstyles, tattoos, earrings, belts etc. What may seem outlandish to you is the general trend amongst children at that time. It is advisable to let children experiment, but within reason. You may disallow the child to colour his/her hair yellow, green or red but a shirt with loud flowers of these colours shouldn't be a problem.

For optimal personality development and social growth children need to be part of a group. Their acceptance into the group will be easier if they look, dress and behave like the rest of the members. If the group comprises of children who are generally well intentioned and don't indulge in any vices or antisocial activities, it should be your endeavour that the child becomes a part of it. The exposure and experimentation within the group would prove to be an useful learning experience for later life.

5. Add Accomplishments-Gain Friends

Children, who are good at swimming, dancing, debating or dramatics, generally get a platform to display their talents. All these activities involve several other children and provide opportunities to interact with each other. **Children who have common interests become special friends**. They learn the virtues of teamwork and with each new success their confidence gets boosted.

A bent for football, basketball, singing or playing an

instrument may never emerge unless the child has a chance to try it. Parents should expose their children to several such opportunities and then help them to pursue the ones for which they have flair. Any interest the child takes up will open the doors of friendship for him/her. Accomplishments aid in finding friends and developing friendships.

6. Family Traditions Matter

In many families friends and friendships are not just cherished but revered. These friendships pass through generations and the ties between families keep growing stronger. When Mehul Khanna's son Madhur took up a job in Mumbai, he rang up his friend Udit Verma, asking him to help Madhur get an accommodation. Udit insisted that the boy stay at his home until he found a place for him. It took one full month to find a suitable accommodation for Madhur. Meanwhile he and Utkarsh, Udit's son, got along nicely to keep up the family tradition.

7. Children need examples.

Parents must set an example by remembering birthdays and anniversaries of friends. Parents who plan get-togethers and outings with friends give their children the message that friendships are important. Children generally pick up the ways of their parents and are likely to be successful in their own friendships. They will always have a group of close, dependable friends to fall back on in times of crisis.

8. No coercion please!

Parents should understand that social needs of children differ. Some children are perfectly happy having one or two close friends, while others are always surrounded by mates. An intelligent, creative child who loves reading or music may find too many friends a bother. Coaxing such a child to make friends will only lead to unnecessary tension. An outgoing child who revels in group activities may have so many engagements that parents will have to force him/her to remain inside the house. This again can lead to a showdown. Whatever your unique situation don't use coercion—persuasion is a far better option.

9. From parent to friend

In time every parent-child relationship should blossom into a warm friendship in which the protagonists interact on a more even keel. By being friends parents can influence and modulate the child's behaviour much more effectively and positively.

The journey from tying your son's shoe laces to letting him try your shoes is a long and taxing one, but it is also one of the most beautiful and fulfilling experiences. Finally a thought for mothers and daughters:

"Spare the stick, share the lipstick"

Some 'Friendly' Suggestions

1. Do not impose unnecessary and unjustified restrictions on your children and their friends. Give them freedom to take independent decisions.

2. Try to know the likes and dislikes of your child's friends. Your familiarity with their passions and liking will win you their trust and respect.
3. Remember to praise the child and his/her friends for their achievements.
4. Children must be taught to inform parents when they are going out, where they are going and when they will come back. Once this habit is inculcated a lot of confusion, anxiety and confrontation can be avoided.
5. If your adolescent son or daughter starts returning home late, gets up late in the morning, doesn't eat well, argues a lot – take this behaviour seriously because it probably denotes association with delinquent boys and a possibility of drug abuse. Seek help from the child's teachers and peers in analysing the situation and taking decisions.
6. Don't ever ridicule the child in front of his/her friends.
7. Talk freely with children. If you withhold information they will acquire misinformation.

17

Smart Parenting

Raising a child is very much like building a skyscraper. If the first few storeys are out of line, no one will notice. But when the building is 18 or 20 storey high, everyone will see that it tilts.

Jim Bishop

How your children grow up will depend not just on the amount of care you give them, or how much money is spent on them, but on how smart a parent you are. The informed status of the parents and their efficiency in tackling everyday situations are the key determinants of children's success.

If you want your children to succeed in life, you have to act with responsibility, restraint, equanimity and patience. You have to be clear and firm while dealing with your children but not at the cost of a warm, loving and mutually gratifying relationship.

Conserve your energy

All of us have a certain amount of physical and mental energy to use in dealing with the everyday activities and stresses of life. Unnecessary conflicts tend to drain our energy.

This means that you have to choose your battlegrounds wisely. Sit down with your child and discuss what you feel are the key issues. Once you have identified them, frame a set of guidelines and channelise your energy to see that they are followed. If you keep reacting to trivial issues, you will have little energy left to deal with the more important problems.

I will try to explain this by equating energy to money. Decide whether an issue is worth Rs.10/-, Rs.100/- or Rs.1000/- then spend your energy in accordance with the importance of the issue. Overspending can only lead to early burnout.

If your child spills a glass of milk think of the following before you start hollering:

1. Was it a mistake? If yes-you don't have any right to shout, even you can make a mistake.
2. Was it deliberate? If yes think about the cost Rs.5/- which is negligible. The only issue worth dealing with is the indiscipline of the child. Talk to him/her and explain the inappropriate behaviour, also warn about the unpleasant consequences in future.

Importance of Saying No

I had gone out for dinner with a family I know very well. As we came out of the restaurant their five year old son **Priyam** saw a hawker selling toy cars. Priyam demanded a particular car and when refused, he started whining, then wailing and finally shrieking with rage. His parents were almost tempted to buy him the car, but their momentary hesitation gave me the opening I was looking for. I told them to deal with the situation firmly and not to succumb to the irrational demand of their child.

On the way back Priyam's cries drowned the car stereo by many a decibel. When I dropped them at their gate his cries had changed to a whimper. I was later informed that Priyam was off to sleep the moment he was put to bed and when he got up in the morning he had forgotten all about the car.

Giving in to a child's demands is the easiest way out—the path of least resistance. But if you do it all the time you will spoil your child. Not only will his/her demands increase; they will become more and more irrational.

Children are the worst victims of advertising blitzkrieg on television. Advertisements for new toys, dolls, chocolates, electronic games and bicycles fire their imagination and increase their cravings. They are easily sold on to new ideas and things and when they are unable to acquire them, they become frustrated. Parents have to guide children to strike a balance between unreasonable demands and reasonable fancies. Here's what you should do:

Money Matters

Don't buy expensive gifts in a casual off-hand manner. If your child wants a new bicycle and you feel it is justified, you should say: "Although you do need a new bicycle, we will have to discuss it. You can't go to the market and pick up a bicycle just like that".

From the very beginning make it clear to your children that whatever you buy for them, or for yourself involves serious decision-making. Also tell them that many things are useless and not worth buying. They must get the message that money is not an unlimited commodity and it must be spent wisely. If you use prudence in indulgence, it will not harm your child.

Don't Feel Guilty

Working parents feel that because they're unable to give sufficient time to their children, they should somehow compensate for their absence. They get into the habit of buying gifts to overcome their feeling of guilt. While this may make the parents feel generous, it is harmful for children as they start demanding gifts and treats all the time.

Don't feel guilty! By working, you are in a position to provide a good living standard, better entertainment and the best education for your child. Instead, try to find time for your child and take interest in his/her interests. Avoid bringing home the files and frustrations of your office.

Stick to your guns

The primary reason why parents give in to their children's

irrational demands is to avoid a 'scene'. Once you say no, it should remain a No! When you deliver a firm No the child gets the message that crying and cajoling will not get him/her anywhere. While saying no you must try to offer the simplest explanation for your refusal.

If your daughter demands a new pair of party shoes and you know she doesn't need them, don't beat about the bush by saying: "they appear quite flimsy, or they are not worth their price, or having so many shoes is unjustified." Such reasoning may sound OK to an adult but it is beyond the comprehension of children. Simply tell her: "you don't need any shoes."

If your child manages to have his/her own way by crying, pleading or pestering, he/she will quickly master the technique and make your life miserable. When the child is creating a scene inside a shop, it is better to let it happen. Stand by your decision, even if your child's 'wailing' makes you look heartless. If necessary catch hold of your child and leave the shop—sometimes you have to be rigid to prove a point.

As parents your job is to help your children decide what's worth getting and what isn't. You should teach them that there are better ways of raising demands and getting them fulfilled. They must learn that throwing themselves on the floor and yelping will not achieve anything.

Be Positive: Remain Optimistic

Parents, who use 'praise' and 'rewards' instead of 'criticism' and 'punishment', generally obtain positive results. They are able to eliminate undesired behaviour and reinforce desired behaviour in their children. Parents must look at the brighter side of the child and highlight his/her competencies and accomplishments. Focussing on the weaknesses and blaming the child for minor lapses can prove to be counter productive.

Yogita, thirteen, was brought to my clinic with the complaints of general weakness and poor memory. She was unable to retain anything and was performing poorly in her studies. Her parents had already administered her a variety of the so-called memory enhancing tonics, but to no effect. While talking to her I was pleasantly surprised by her clear and precise diction. Her parents also confirmed that she always spoke very clearly and with correct pronunciations, even when she was a little girl.

I instinctively enquired whether she had ever participated in a speech or a debate competition—the answer was in the negative. I suggested that she should enter her name whenever an opportunity came her way.

At the end of the consultation I wrote out two prescriptions. Yogita's prescription contained an iron tonic, as she was mildly anaemic. Her parent's prescription was 1. Motivate Yogita to participate in a speech/debate competition. 2. Give her 100% support—emotional as well as material-when she decides to participate.

Two months later a beaming Yogita entered my clinic with her parents. She was holding an impressive looking trophy in her hands she had won in an inter-school speech competition. She stood first among 50 odd children from 18 leading schools of the city. The topic was 'Eliminate

Child Labour'. No doubt, her parents had helped her in writing the speech, but it was Yogita who delivered it with aplomb.

The victory gave a tremendous boost to Yogita's confidence and she developed faith in her abilities. This started reflecting in her improved academic performance as well, and her 'memory problem' became a thing of the past.

Let Children Take Charge

You can't teach 'responsibility' but you can make a child 'responsible'. **Aayush**, twelve, was an incorrigible little brat—lazy, irritable and generally disinterested. He loved to watch just about anything on television and his only contribution in the house was—maintaining it in a state of perpetual mess.

Ultimately his parents decided to involve him in running the household. Aayush was given the responsibility for purchasing monthly grocery. His parents were to guide him in this endeavour. He was given a certain amount of money, equivalent to average monthly expenditure on grocery, at the beginning of the month. He was also provided with a diary to maintain the record of purchases. If any money was left at the end of the month, it went to his kitty.

Today Aayush has no time for television – he is a busy young businessman. He has learned to save and to spend wisely. His arithmetic marks and his bank balance both have improved substantially.

Practice what you preach

One of the most significant ways children learn what to do and what not to do is by watching their parents. So be careful, you are their first and foremost role model-sooner or later they will imitate your actions and behaviour.

If you shout to get your way, expect your children to do the same. If you remain sprawled on a sofa watching television instead of finishing urgent household chores, your children will also learn to defer doing their homework. If you want to inculcate reading habits in your child, start reading yourself. If you want your child to say sorry and thank you, better start using these words yourself. When your child sees you apologising for a mistake he/she will quickly learn to do the same.

Heads I win—tails you lose

Choose two options that are both acceptable to you, then ask the child to decide which one of the two he/she prefers. Whatever the child's decision, it leaves you happy and smiling. For example, ask the child whether he/she would like to study in the night for the exam or will he/she get up early in the morning. Either way you ensure that your child prepares for the exam. If instead of 'either' the child replies 'neither', remind him/her that 'neither' is not an option and he/she has to choose from the two offered options. Just hold on to your nerves, your child will make a choice within a few minutes.

If you adopt an open-ended approach and ask the child: "When would you like to study for your exam?"—

You may either get no response or one that is not acceptable to you. Smart parents make it appear that it is the child who is making the choice.

Don't play Sherlock Holmes

You return home from work and switch on the TV for latest news—the screen remains dark. Your latest acquisition, a 29" flat screen television set, which you left in perfect working condition in the morning, has conked out. You call over your children and pointing to the TV thunder, "Who did it?" Your children will vehemently deny coming anywhere near the television. It will be almost impossible to find out, "Who did it", as they will keep blaming each other.

Children are driven by curiosity and spirit of adventure. If and when this turns into a 'misadventure' simply depends upon your bad luck. The question "Who did it", creates a situation where the child feels cornered and the fear of punishment makes him/her point an accusing finger at a sibling or a servant. By asking 'who' you convey that your intention is to find out and punish the guilty. Whether the child has done it or not he/she will usually answer, "not me", and try to shift the blame on others.

If, instead of "Who did it", you ask. "How did it happen", you will have a better chance of getting a response. Call your children and point out the problem. If they accuse each other, tell them you are not interested in knowing who did it, but in knowing why the television is not working. Your children are sure to feel bad about damaging the TV, and are likely to be more responsible in future. Finally, it may turn out that your TV has a blown fuse, and there was absolutely no need for you to have blown your fuse as well.

Avoid being a super parent

Apoorv was launched on the path of success from the moment his umbilical cord was cut. When he was a little baby, his father fortified him with a multitude of multivitamin syrups, while his mother tried to strengthen his body by massaging him with pure olive oil.

Now his parents strive hard to ensure that he always comes first, whether it is academics, sports, dancing, painting, singing or debating. While talking to Apoorv their favourite words are: vital, urgent, significant, important, at the end of the day. They ferry him to endless tutions and coaching throughout the day. The evenings are again devoted to achieving academic excellence.

Yes! Apoorv's parents are 'Super Parents' and they want him to be a 'Super Kid'. They have unlimited energy and they are so highly charged that they just can't relax. Their devotion towards the success of their child can give an inferiority complex to us 'ordinary', 'normal' parents. By seeing them operate—at full throttle, always—we may sometimes be forced to verify our antecedents and credentials as good parents.

Super parents are so busy running and doing things for their children, that they miss out on just being with their children. They get trapped in their own frantic drive to succeed and fail to forge an emotional and mental bonding with their children. By their exacting standards and demands for perfection they put extreme pressure on their children, who start feeling guilty and unworthy if they fail to live up to the super expectations of their super parents. Thus unknowingly they make their children anxious and unhappy.

Some people may argue in favor of 'Super Parents', but they should sit back and think a while! Who is being benefited from all these efforts? Are you making your child miserable because of your own needs for glory? Is he/she being sacrificed at the altar of your ego? If yes, then perhaps its time for you to drop the façade of being a 'Super Parent' and begin sincere efforts at becoming a 'Normal Parent'.

Learn to Breathe Easy

Children will make mistakes; they will do silly, mischievous or thoughtless things. Parents must maintain their cool. When parents tend to forget their own childhood—its trails and its joys, things get complicated. Take a few deep breaths and try to calm down. It's hard to think clearly when you're angry and you might forget every sensible thing you know about good parenting. *One of the very best ways to become better parents is to batter your anger and not your child.*

18

Are You a Good Father?

It is easier for a father to have children than for children to have a real father.
                                                    Pope John xxiii

Even though mothers interact with children the most, the father's influence on the social growth and behaviour of children is substantial. The father influences his children's behaviour in a variety of direct and indirect ways. His personal-social values provide the foundation on which his children build their future lives. He influences the mother's attitudes towards home and child management.

In most homes father constitutes the court of highest appeal whenever a disciplinary crisis erupts. Even in his absence his larger-than-life image helps the mother to remain in control. Sentences beginning with: "Let your father come home then ———" or "I'll tell your dad about ———" remain popular weapons in the arsenal of mothers even in the twenty-first century.

As far as boys are concerned, the father serves not only as a role model but also as the principal source of disciplinary control. This inevitably leads to frustration, which results in aggressive tendencies directed against siblings and peers. Girls, on the other hand, appear to have few conflicts with their fathers. Most of their tussles and contests are with their mothers. This however does not mean that the father's behaviour is not important to his daughter's psychological development. In fact most fathers affect both their daughter s and son's psychosocial adjustments in equal proportions.

It has been observed that children separated from their fathers tend to develop high levels of anxiety. This is evidenced in their fears and nightmares, in their conflicts with peers and in poor academic performance. These children lack warmth and affection for anyone but their mothers. They have hostile feelings for others, but they may not express them in overt aggressive acts. Repression of hostility can lead to frustration and further increase in anxiety levels.

Ideally both parents should contribute equally in the running of household, but this generally does not happen. The homes are either mother or father dominated. In matriarchal homes the father's role is marginal and his presence—incidental. It can be assumed that his influence on children's personality development and social growth is negligible. In patriarchal homes, a dominating father may adversely affect his child's personality and achievements. Fathers, who are involved with their children in a non dominating and non-interfering way, usually succeed in motivating their children to achieve desired goals.

The father's influence within the home is decisive in many aspects of child rearing. Most fathers have very definite aspirations and hopes regarding the behaviour of their sons and daughters. They want their sons to be obedient, responsible and masculine. They hope their sons would show initiative, some degree of aggressiveness, good academic achievement, and move towards a satisfying and profitable career. As far as daughters are concerned they would like them to be gentle, affectionate and marriageable. With changing times the difference in the treatment of sons and daughters has reduced considerably, especially in the educated middle class homes. Education and career of girls is now given equal, if not more, importance than boys.

How to be a good 'Pa'

1. Express your love

When **Alisha's** parents returned home from work they noticed that their nine-year-old daughter was not her usual chirpy, bubbly self. She looked dull, dejected and dispirited and was wandering around the house aimlessly. When her worried parents questioned her, she broke down but kept on shaking her head saying, "It's nothing."

Finally her father sat down with her, took her hand and tenderly questioned her until he learnt the cause of her sadness. Alisha had practised hard; she had memorised all her lines. Yet her teacher had removed her from the play to be staged on the annual day. Gently, simply, Alisha's father talked to her of life, opportunity, striving and success. He comforted her. He didn't dismiss the episode as trivial but treated her with dignity and concern.

Alisha's father was expressing love for his daughter, giving her his time and trying to see the world through her eyes and from her perspective.

No doubt! You love your child, but find it difficult to show it. Don't lose heart, this is a common ailment among fathers. If you feel you have problems expressing affection, make special efforts: write it in a letter or give a card which says what you always wanted to say but couldn't because of your inhibitions. You can write an admiring note on the back of one of your child's drawings. I myself can't be called a very demonstrative father, but my skills at writing poetry, has kept me in business. My daughters may not think I am a great poet but they do feel that the poems I write for them are a true expression of my love.

Most children wish their fathers would tell or show them in some way, that they really love them. Many adults concede that they can't recall their fathers ever hugging or kissing them or saying they loved them. Illnesses probably are the only occasions when fathers allow the clouds of indifference to clear and let their concern shine through.

Some children feel uncomfortable with public displays of affection, especially when friends are around. Make no mistake, they need your love and encouragement but in a subtle, covert manner. When your child is about to participate in a sports activity or perform on the stage you can use a thumbs up sign to indicate your support and faith in his/her capabilities.

Generally children are quite expressive and open in showing their love. They may cuddle up to you, put their arms around your neck or simply climb on your back as if testing both—the strength of your back and your love. When your child says: "I love you dad," surely, you feel on top of the world. So why don't you also express your love and help your child conquer the world.

As a father you can show your love in many ways. If you show respect, affection and concern for your wife, you indirectly convey the same feelings for your children. Apparent affection and harmony between parents is the most reassuring sight for children.

Find time for your children

You may be very busy making mega-deals, conceptualising and implementing huge projects but don't do it at the cost of neglecting your children. When you are back home don't push away your children saying, "Leave me alone". You can't make a worse investment for future. Remember time and love are the two most important things your kids need and desire from you. It is not always necessary for you to talk, your simple presence and crisp 'yes' and 'no' to their queries is sufficient for them to feel at peace.

If you are working in the garden, call over your children—not for help but to listen to their banter and to share your day. If you are working on the computer and there are no deadlines to be met, let your child operate the mouse for a while and later appreciate his/her help. Sometimes I sit down on the dining table to write, and ask my daughters to come and sit with me to finish their homework. They do disturb me, but it is a small price to pay for their companionship and the label of a considerate father.

There are hoards of activities to get involved in. You can play indoor/outdoor games or go cycling, trekking or fishing. All children love kite flying—use this opportunity to form a team with your child. If both parents are working the family should at least have dinner together.

Fathers who have to do a lot of travelling on the job or who are in armed forces/merchant navy and have to be away from home for prolonged periods, should try to maintain constant contact with their children. They can ring up or write frequent letters to keep the relationship blossoming.

Lack of paternal supervision has been related to lower IQ and poor academic performance. Children from such homes show a high incidence of violent behaviour and delinquency. They are also more prone to drug addictions. Paternal involvement is vital to all round personality development in a child.

Few years back parents were sold the concept of 'Quality Time'. They were told that thirty minutes of focussed, uninterrupted, playful interaction with the child was better than spending an entire uneventful evening together. This concept was probably the brainchild of people who anyway didn't have much time for their children. Now again it is being gradually recognised that quantity does matter. Moreover, you can't plan quality time and tell your child: "OK! Sit tight and smile, your quality time starts now!"

Actually it is the routine tasks like—driving your children to school, helping them with their assignments or putting them to bed, which should be converted into special moments.

View things from the child's perspective

Don't expect the child to think and behave like an adult. Try to recall your own childhood and what you liked and what you didn't. Fathers who overlook the child's point of view generally fail to build a bond of mutual trust and understanding.

Dr. Mishra, an ENT Surgeon, remembers taking his seven-year old son **Piyush** to a cricket match. It was supposed to be a great father-son experience as they watched the match together. Thirty minutes into the game Piyush announced, "I am getting bored. Let's go home now". It had not occurred to Dr. Mishra that a seven-year-old could view the great Indian pastime with anything but enthusiasm. He tried to get his son interested by telling him funny anecdotes about the game of cricket. He took out the thermos and offered him tea, but nothing worked. Soon, an angry father and a bored son trooped out of the stadium.

Driving home Dr. Mishra cooled down, probably the cool breeze helped. On an impulse he took a detour and stopped in front of the National Science Museum building. Piyush had been to the Museum once with his class and was eager to go again. Father and son went from exhibit to exhibit, and each time Piyush made a discovery he gleefully shared it with his father. The day is etched sharply in Dr. Mishra's memory because on this day he learnt—it was fun to see the world through his son's eyes.

Move with times

As compared to mothers, fathers generally tend to become outdated earlier. So keep your eyes wide open and ears finely tuned for 'change'. From being a toddler, to becoming a teenager your child makes rapid progress. You must also move with times and keep in touch with your child's changing tastes. You should be well informed about the recent trends in clothing, food-fads and teenage-lingo (slang). Remember! Children are very prompt in labeling their fathers as ancient/vintage.

A conservative doctor friend of mine was quite upset with the dress sense of his gawky, teenaged daughter. Her bare-dare attire and dazzling make up was enough to blind any parent with fury. When he looked around he found that most girls of her age were more or less similarly dressed in skimpy, body hugging dresses. Rather than admonishing her, my friend figured that by aping them, his daughter was simply trying to be part of her peer group. By making a fashion statement and by her flair for wisecracks she not only became a part of the gang but in fact was leading it.

During the annual club dinner our families happened

to share the same table. Even though my friend's daughter was wearing her usual tight black dress and a terrifying luminescent eye shadow, her behaviour was exemplary. She chatted with us with confidence and even entertained us with her funny remarks about the 'best dancing couple of the eve'.

I am sure in a few years time she will become more responsible and prove to be a successful young lady. Her father's confidence in her and acceptance of her as she was were the two most important factors in building her confidence and self-esteem. Criticism and rejection by her father would surely have alienated her, damaged her personality and given her an inferiority complex.

The applauding father

Any achievement or victory, big or small, needs to be recognised and appreciated wholeheartedly. I still vividly remember my father giving a big party in recognition of my scoring good grades in board-examinations. He introduced me to all his friends during the party—his smile reaching his eyes and his hand constantly patting my back. I felt wonderful. My father gave me a sense of self-confidence that has never left me. The power of a father's encouraging words is truly immense.

It's natural for fathers to cheer the success of their sons but their support and appreciation is even more vital to the success of their daughters. It has been seen that successful women usually have fathers who back them and encourage them in all their endeavours. They see their daughters as future achievers and never let them feel that they can't do certain things because they are girls.

The reliable father

- A good father doesn't make promises he can't keep.
- A reliable father delivers even when he hasn't promised.

The role of a father as a mere provider is no more acceptable. Although giving financial security still remains his primary responsibility, active involvement in the day to day affairs of children is the trademark of a good father.

If your child wants you to attend a school play, a game or some other event important to him—be there if you have promised. Of course you can't be present on all such occasions but give the child a convincing answer for your inability to attend. The daughter of a senior sales executive wanted her father to be present at the prize distribution ceremony of her school because she was to receive the best swimmer's award. Her father skipped an important business meeting to be present at the function, even though he had not promised. When she was called on the stage to receive her trophy and saw her father standing near the stage clapping, her face lit up and her trophy appeared to shine brighter.

The reasonable father

Fathers who approach conflicts with an open mind and a flexible attitude generally come up with amicable solutions. Those who have the additional virtue of patience convert this process of solution-finding into an exercise for strengthening relationships with those they love.

A friend's daughter wanted to go on a trekking trip, which also involved mountain climbing. He refused saying: "You are too young and it could be dangerous." After a brief standoff the conflict was resolved and the father agreed to talk to the organisers of the trip. He came back convinced that the people organising the trek were thorough professionals and his dear daughter would be safe with them. The daughter received a certificate of trekking while the father earned a bond of everlasting love and understanding.

Follow some endearing rituals

Children love picnics and outings with their fathers, but they are equally happy doing things with them around the house. Fathers can make their children feel special by following some simple rituals. Bed time stories, a game of cards or simply talking and laughing together before going off to sleep, all give children a wonderful sense of well being. They never forget these gestures of love and companionship and cherish them throughout their lives.

Many fathers find it difficult to tell stories. The simplest and the best thing to do is to talk about the family's past. This helps to develop a feeling of family togetherness. All children love to hear what they were like as babies. Were they naughty or good. Who cared for them, who fed them, what did they eat—there is enough material for stories inside every home.

Dare to discipline

There will be occasions when despite the mother's commanding presence the father will have to administer the bitter pill of discipline to the child. Almost all parents concede to using some form of physical punishment while disciplining their children. It never creates a rift between them. It is only when children are arbitrarily punished or abused that the problems arise.

There is an old Chinese tale about a father whose son had taken to lying. Each time he was caught in the act, he would promise never to lie again but with each passing day he lied more and more until one day his father decided to discipline him. The father caught hold of the son and put him atop a high wooden almirah. He asked his son to promise never to lie again or keep sitting on the almirah. As was his habit, the son promptly promised not to lie again, without ever meaning it. 'OK!' Said his father: "Jump down, I promise I'll catch you." The son hesitated for a moment but when his father repeated the promise, he jumped down. The father moved back and the son landed on the floor with an almighty crash.

"Do you ever want me to lie to you again?" asked the father.

"No father," replied the son. According to the story the son never lied again, neither to his father, nor to anyone else.

Make a team with your wife

Successful running of any household depends upon good teamwork between husband and wife. They need to agree on a set of house rules and then ensure that they are followed. A husband must always back up his wife while dealing with indiscipline.

Some fathers try to ingratiate themselves with their children by allowing them to do forbidden things in the absence of their wives. Some even go to the extent of making fun and running down their wives. Fathers who play this game of one-upmanship generally end up as losers. It also holds true for mothers. If a mother thinks her husband is not good enough, her children will also feel the same. On the contrary a "Dad" rated number one by "Mum", is usually given the same rating by her children.

Don't shirk housework

Father's contribution in housework has always been and still remains a contentious issue. Generally the entire responsibility of running the household lies with the mother, even though she may herself be in a full time job. Winds of change are gathering momentum and there is a perceptible difference in the attitudes of new generation.

Today many men actively share the responsibilities of parenthood with their wives. To them preparing feed for the baby is as important as readying a project report. I am quite sure my father never changed a nappy in his entire fatherhood, but I am quite adept at it. I must have changed hundreds of wet nappies of my two daughters. My wife has always been quite appreciative of the fact and is of the firm belief that all females should preferably marry pediatricians.

A father who is a good cook is like a knight in shining

armour. When he is in the kitchen cooking one of his delicacies the entire family joins in to help. Can there be a stronger glue to bind the family together? Sons of such fathers are likely to master the culinary skills and become 'special fathers' themselves.

You don't have to be a master-chef to be a good father. You can begin by boiling eggs and later on graduate to making omelets, sandwiches and shakes. If you can't accomplish these tasks, don't lose heart, there are other avenues to show your mettle. You can clear or lay the table, take things out from the fridge and heat them, fill the water bottles and ice trays—the list is endless. By seeing you help your wife in the kitchen your children will also be motivated to learn those chores.

Some fathers have a technical bent of mind and an aptitude for fixing things. Your children will love to join you while you repair a leaking tap or a blown fuse. I would advice you to spend five minutes during weekends to oil and grease your child's bicycle. He will love it!

Share your problems

In this competitive, materialistic world tension and anxiety are the two most common baggage that any successful man has to carry. If you have a problem—you are being transferred or there is a danger of your losing your job, don't hide it from your family. Children are quick to sense when parents are troubled and this can give rise to apprehension and insecurity. It's best to be candid with children. Utilise this opportunity to bring the family closer. Let children know the family is strong enough to tide over any crisis. You'll be surprised by their resilience and capacity to cope.

No father is perfect. Good fathers are those who work hard to develop the qualities that strengthen family life. They devote equal time to both—building their careers and building their relationship, especially with their children. I have described home as the base-camp, mother remains it's undisputed base-commander and the father is second-in-command. Being a father myself, I know—we can't replace mothers.

19

Teachers Teach-Hobbies Educate

I have never let my schooling interfere with my education

Mark Twain

Every child has immense potential and several unearthed talents. Opportunities or the lack of them can either make or mar a child's future prospects. While there is no denying the importance of formal education, hobbies play no less a part in the education of a child. They help to channelise the boundless energy that children have and provide openings for the fulfillment of true potential.

I still hang my favourite suit on the 'steel-hanger' I made myself when studying in Class VIII. The magazine-stand, which I fabricated with the help of my 'metal-work' teacher, continues to hold my magazines. I had the good fortune of studying in a school where emphasis was equally distributed between academic and co-curricular activities. If your child's school doesn't offer facilities for all-round personality development, try to take the responsibility for the same. Let teachers teach, meanwhile continue and augment the child's education at home by introducing him/her to various hobbies.

New interests and pursuits have the capacity to bring alive and excite our sleeping brain cells. They also act as safety valves and help in releasing the pent-up anxiety and tension. The sense of achievement associated with hobbies gives us happiness and satisfaction. It motivates us to pursue and attain our goals successfully.

Anything and everything can be picked up as a hobby. Expensive hobbies are not necessarily more rewarding. Children love to collect stones, which doesn't cost anything. You can use the stones to teach the child about shapes, sizes, and colours and maybe later about how rocks are formed.

Adolescence is the age when human creativity comes to the fore. Parents must try to assess the child's potential and special interests at their own level. Adolescent imagination, inquisitiveness and exuberance—needs to be directed into constructive endeavours. Some children manifest aptitude and skills in more than one area. Their multi-dimensional personalities provide them with many achievements and a succession of victories. Their life is like a beautiful bouquet containing bright flowers of varied colours.

Listing of all hobbies is neither feasible nor intended

because the exercise will always remain incomplete. However, three basic interests which are extremely useful in building an all-round personality, need some elaboration. These three key hobbies are:
1. Reading.
2. Travel.
3. Stage.

Reading

Reading and studying are two entirely different pursuits and should not be confused. While a person could prefer reading anything from a comic strip to a dictionary; studying involves the onerous and mostly tedious job of going through the subject matter with an eye on the exams. Schools and exams are a necessary part of our educational system, with which every child has to grapple with in order to get into a satisfying career. If parents are able to inculcate wider reading habits in their wards, that's where the real knowledge comes from.

There is no denying the fact that with the growing burden of academic curriculum and yearly increments in the weight of the school bag (rather than the child), children are gradually but surely being alienated from books. To add to it, the relentless onslaught of innumerable TV channels kills whatever little interest children are able to develop in reading. Many parents complain that their children don't read at all. Instead of blaming children we should help them pick up a nice, interesting book. Once the habit is acquired, reading becomes a source of extreme enjoyment and books become the best of friends.

To develop reading habits the presence of plenty of books is a must. Gift children books at every opportunity, take them to libraries and book-fairs. Let them touch, feel and hold books. Gradually they will fall in love with them, and this is one love affair where there is no looking back.

Merely giving books is not enough; parents must involve themselves with the child's reading activities. The first step is to read to the child from his/her books. Once the child has learnt to read you can ask him/her to read to you his/her favourite stories. With older children parents should try to discuss the book they have recently read, its narrative and the usage of words. You can ask them to suggest an alternate ending to a story and give your opinion regarding it.

Just as you need proteins, carbohydrates and fats for a healthy body you require good books for a healthy mind. Books are like Vitamins; they improve the quality of life. While introducing children to books parents must take precaution that they are not loaded with uninteresting and incomprehensible stuff, because this will surely kill their interest at the initial stage itself. Parents must also keep track of the child's reading habits and the type of books he/she reads. Adolescents can fall prey to the lure of undesirable magazines and books, which may damage their psychosocial development.

Travel

When one sees a thing with one's own eyes it becomes permanently stamped in the memory. This is the easiest and the most effective way of acquiring knowledge. To widen their intellectual horizons, children must be exposed directly to various sources of knowledge and information. Children are naturally curious and when their queries are solved by showing them the things as they really are and not through 'poorly brought out' text books they are better able to understand and retain the information.

A child may memorise his/her history lessons but they will soon be forgotten. A teacher may struggle hard but the child will neither be able to understand 'Mughal' architecture nor appreciate the grandeur of Red Fort, Fatehpur Sikri or The Taj Mahal. It's not just the historical monuments, a widely traveled child has a wider area of interest and a greater pool of knowledge.

Travelling/Tourism is the best manner of educating a child. It not only gives pleasure but also stimulates the imagination and thought process of an individual. Whatever his/her age, take your child on outdoor trips and various sightseeing tours. There is so much to explore in and around each and every city. There are rivers, lakes, forests and hills to be seen. There are historical monuments, ancient buildings and museums to be visited. There are factories, dams and power stations to learn from.

Children, who are given ample travel opportunities— with family, school trips, NCC camps–tend to be physically and mentally stronger. They learn to rough it out from an early age. They become adept at surviving without the comforts available to them at home. These traits come in handy when these children grow up and leave home to take on the world.

It's a good idea to ask children to write down their experiences when they come back from a tour. If it was a trip involving several children—cousins/friends – organise an essay competition titled 'My Trip' at the end and give handsome prizes to the winners. This helps children to articulate their thoughts and may even motivate them to find out more about the places and monuments they visited. The knowledge thus acquired broadens their perspective and makes them more confident.

Stage

The school stage is like miniature art form, which prepares the child to paint successfully on the full canvas of life. Stage provides opportunities to demonstrate various latent talents and skills. Motivate children to take interest in and participate in stage activities from an early age. A successful sojourn on stage generates feelings of accomplishment and boosts self-image. Successive stage success builds confidence and allows the child to face the world with assurance.

Stage fright is not an uncommon entity. Many capable and highly intelligent persons find themselves totally helpless when asked to come on stage. The inability to face an audience and express thoughts and views boldly remains a major handicap in many people's life. Whether it's an oral exam or an interview for a job, the candidate who walks in confidently and speaks with conviction usually gets through.

Children who can sing, play an instrument, act,

compere or those who participate in debates, speech competitions, poetry recitation are the ones who occupy centrestage in school. Teachers recognise them and peers admire them.

With changing times the spectrum of career options has also changed and widened a lot. Today several young men and women are choosing modelling, television, films and stage as their profession. Even otherwise, individuals who were active on stage during their formative years succeed in conventional jobs also. Their ability to speak eloquently and the confidence which they had acquired while facing large gatherings comes in handy when dealing with subordinates, colleagues and superiors.

Whether it is a neighbourhood cultural activity, a school function or an even bigger competition, parents must help their child to get onto the stage. When enough opportunities are provided, the child is bound to become stage savvy. Once the child learns to be confident on stage he/she will automatically be confident in other areas of life.

Finally let's take a look at some common hobbies and how they facilitate the learning process. An individual can pick up one or more hobbies, it all depends upon the aptitude and capabilities of the person concerned. As we grow our interests and hobbies may change, the important thing is to maintain our enthusiasm and curiosity for new things in life. Gerhart Hauptmann said, "Once you have become a master in a thing, you should become a pupil in something new".

S.No.	Hobby	Educative Component + Other Benefits
1.	Stamp and coin collection	Acquisition of information regarding various countries, important people and events.
2.	Drawing and Painting	Ability to draw good diagrams, strengthening of creative skills and drives.
3.	Judo, Karate	Disciplined, systematic and confident approach to life.
4.	Team games	Learning the elements of co-operation and teamwork.
5.	Singing, Dance, Musical Instruments	Improves concentration, confidence and popularity.
6.	Writing poems, stories etc.	Better expression and improved vocabulary.
7.	Photography/Videography	Augmentation of conceptualisation and imagination.
8.	Gardening	Learning about plants and nature.
9.	Cookery, Home decoration	Add to the child's ever growing list of accomplishments.
10.	Computers, Internet	The impact is mind-boggling.

20

Reach For The Moon

A child is not a vase to be filled, but a fire to be lit.
                                                    Rabelais

Until Neil Armstrong set foot on it, the moon had remained confined to fairy tales or served as a source of inspiration for poets. The success of Apollo-11 expedition is a saga of human ingenuity, striving, tenacity and determination. It teaches us that unless you aim high, you'll never reach the top.

A quotation by Bill Eardley says it all, "Ambition is the path to success. Persistence is the vehicle you arrive in." All success-stories are made up of two vital ingredients:

1. The desire to succeed.
2. The doggedness of purpose.

An achievement–oriented child has developed conscience; his/her sense of control comes from within. For this condition to come about, it is necessary for the child to look upon one or both his/her parents as 'achievers'. Parents must convey to the child that his/her success is important as well as valuable to them. Once this happens, the child will start worrying about his/her academic performance and other achievements. Unconsciously he/she starts competing with his/her parents, and tries to better their accomplishments. In fact, it should also be the aim of parents that their children do better than themselves in life.

If we view things in a wider perspective we will find that societies which place a premium on achievers, become economic powers. Parental attitudes and child rearing practices not only play an important role in the success of the child but also in building up a society in which many individuals strive together for achievement and economic development. The following three conditions have a positive correlation with the entrepreneurial levels of individuals and societies:
- Motivation and training for achievement by parents at home.
- Frequency of achievement themes in folk tales, story books and school curricula.
- General social approval of success and disapproval of failure.

Goals are a must, they enable children to actualise their powers and personalities.

Goallessness is a curse, which exposes the individual to ridicule and rejection of the family, friends and society alike.

Parents cannot and should not decide the child's goal. However, they must play an active role in:
- Setting of the goal.
- Planning the strategy.
- Execution of the plan.

During all these three stages 'personality profile' of the child should be kept in mind:
- Aptitude and liking.
- Talent and skills.
- Resourcefulness and strengths.

The cascading effect of realistic versus unrealistic goals

Parenting is an art, which relies heavily on the use of common sense in bringing up successful kids. All parents can claim to possess the five special senses, namely— ability to hear, see, smell, taste and touch. But how many of us can vouch for having the sixth, all-important one, 'the common sense'. It indeed is a scarce commodity.

In these times of fierce competition when everybody is trying to 'snatch' the cake, 'kidnap' the baker and 'hijack' the bakery, it is the sixth sense, which helps one survive and succeed. Parents have to use their common sense and their experience of having faced life and its vagaries in helping children decide their goal. Realistic goals can make the child a winner, while setting of unrealistic goals can only lead to frustration and failure.

Both, realistic and unrealistic goals have a cascading effect. While the former lead to success, the latter are a cause of doom.

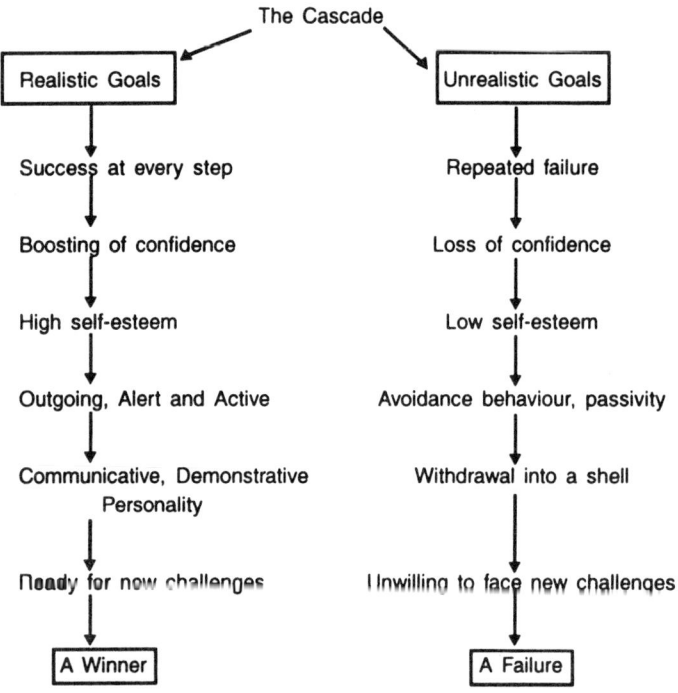

How to reach for the Moon

Some children are highly focussed and goal oriented from a very young age. Parents of such children are lucky in the sense that they only have to facilitate the child's efforts through proper guidance. However, most children only have a vague idea of what they want to achieve. Parental guidance in such cases has to be supplemented with motivation, planning and execution of strategies to attain success.

Generally, academic excellence is the primary goal for a vast majority of children and parents. A range of nonconventional careers have opened up innumerable opportunities for children in the 21st century. Whatever the child's goal, parents must ensure that it is stamped indelibly on his/her mind.

To achieve success in any field, basic principles remain the same. Let's discuss some important ones:

1. Parents must help the child to define his/her goal clearly and realistically. Initially they should stimulate the child to think where he/she wants to get in life. They should constantly interact with the child to eliminate all fuzziness of thought and ask him/her to be precise in his/her decision. Once this basic objective has been met they should help the child to formulate and write the goal in a sharp clear statement. Paste the written goal in the child's room prominently:

   - I want to top in the class.
   - I want to be the school captain.
   - I want to be in the state cricket/tennis/basketball team.
   - I want to be a designer/architect/doctor/software engineer.

2. The goal should be broken into several smaller goals so that there is a sense of achievement at every step. This is a necessary precaution to keep the child focussed on the ultimate target.

3. Motivate the child to study and learn all that he/she can about the goal and how to get there.

4. Fixing a time frame for achieving the goal is of utmost importance. It helps to optimise the utilisation of time and paves the way for time bound success.

5. Do it today. Don't leave things for tomorrow because tomorrow never arrives. Each 'tomorrow' becomes 'today' the next day. So in any case you will have to do it 'today'-why not do it now! Look at it, this way- if you live to be seventy years of age, you will have just 25, 550 days. If we take ten years to fifty years as an individual's most productive period, that leaves only 14,600 days to achieve the goal. So each day is important, use it well.

6. Keep counting minutes and hours. Once you have set a goal and written it down, engage yourself in thinking and planning for its attainment. Decide how much time, you'll give each day towards achieving your goal. It's better to keep the 'work schedule' flexible. Just see to it that daily target is achieved with sincerity and regularity.

The Goal Planner

Goal: To score more than 90% marks in Board Examination.

Name: Prakhar Shrivastava Effort: 6 Hours of study daily.

Date	Time	Duration in hours	Total	Remarks
19.11.2001	2.30 to 4.30 pm	2		
	5.00 to 7.00 pm	2	6.30	Excellent
	8.00 to 9.00 pm	1		
	10.00 to 11.30 pm	1.30		
20.11.2001	6.00 to 7.00 am	1		
	3.00 to 4.00 pm	1	4.00	Poor
	5.00 to 6.00 pm	1		
	8.00 to 9.00 pm	1		

Excellent: Exceeding the target
Good: Meeting the target
Poor: Failing the target

7. Persuade the child to give his/her complete and unremitting effort towards achieving the goal and to never give up trying. Parent's endeavour should be to prevent the child from losing focus, otherwise all the effort and planning would go in vain. Labour along with your child and keep pushing him/her towards the goal.

8. If there is some setback or negative thoughts enter the child's mind, induce him/her into applying positive thinking. Help the child to keep learning, growing and improving.

9. Believers are achievers. Children who do not believe they can achieve success tend not to succeed. Those who believe in themselves are able to maximise their strengths and minimise their deficiencies. Parents can turn their children into believers by carefully nurturing their self-esteem.

10. Remember there are no shortcuts to achieving a goal. Shortcuts may give you a temporary victory, but they can neither give a sense of security nor of achievement. The castles built through such means collapse at the beginning of first storm. Make children strike a balance between physical, mental and emotional striving. A person, who can maintain his/her balance, successfully completes the tightrope walk of life.

11. The children have to be told that the ladder to attaining any goal has only three rungs—
- Determination
- Dedication
- Discipline

12. The failure Triad

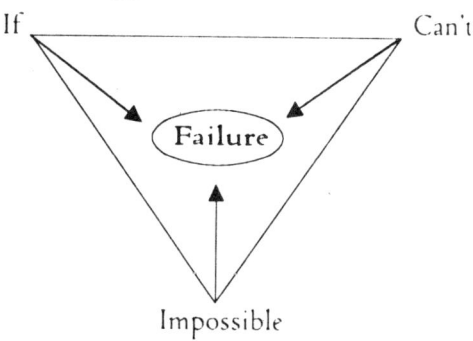

Remove 'If, 'Can't', 'Impossible' and every other negative world from your and child's vocabulary. Negative words generate feelings of helplessness and lead to failure. Replace negative thoughts with positive attitudes:
- Why not
- Can do
- It is possible

13. The Achievement Triangle.

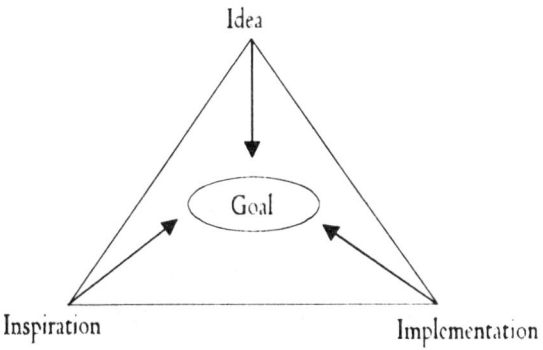

It is only during moments of 'inspiration' that one gets a great 'idea'. Latching on to it and assimilating it as one's goal is the next step. 'Implementation' of strategies to achieve the goal is the final act. So many people who fail or who could have done a terrific job in life but couldn't- lack the initiative to do it. They may get an idea, but they don't put in a wholehearted effort and don't let their entire self become involved in its implementation. They do not fail; they only give up trying.

Don'ts

1. Do not take a shot at your goal without preparing to the fullest.
2. Do not approach the goal with negative thoughts clouding your mind.
3. Do not change your goal midway on whims and fancies of self or others.
4. Do not refuse outside help and guidance in the quest of your goal.
5. Do not try to rush towards your goal—slow and steady usually wins the race.
6. Do not lose your patience, confidence and fortitude.
7. Do not create enemies or generate animosity en-route to your goal.
8. Do not rest on your laurels; keep trying for further excellence. Once a goal has been achieved fix a new one. Keep increasing the degree of difficulty. Gradually success will become a habit.